In Heaven's Eyes

Kimberly A. Snipe

Flint, MI
USA

ISBN Paperback: 9780578995632

Printed in the United States of America.

TABLE OF CONTENTS

Introduction, Dedication, Acknowlegements

Chapter One ....Page 9
In The Beginning

Chapter Two..Page 19
Sweet Memories

Chapter Three..Page 25
Says Who?

Chapter Four..Page 37
There's Hope

Chapter Five..Page 45
Fought a Good Battle

Chapter Six..Page 59
A New Life

Chapter Seven..Page 69
College Journey

Chapter Eight...Page 86
If Only He Knew

Chapter Nine..Page 92
Summertime

Chapter Ten..Page 104
Our Gatherings

Chapter Eleven..Page 117
Now What?!?

Chapter Twelve..Page 132
I Do or I Don't

Chapter Thirteen..Page 151
I Am a D.O.R.K./ You Are Worthy

Chapter Fourteen...Page 160
What's The Point? How Does This Apply to You?

Chapter Fifteen..Page 179
Final Thoughts?

Introduction

From hopelessness to hope, from darkness to light, from shame to confidence, and from fear to faith! *In Heaven's Eyes* you will be taken on an exciting journey…a journey that will provide you with a heavenly glimpse of how God turned things around in my life as a young Deaf girl growing up. After seeing what God has done for me in my life, I totally believe with all my heart that He will do the same for you, if you open your heart, your mind and be willing to hear Him.

Our awesome Heavenly Father has graciously promised to us in Deuteronomy 31:6, to "Be strong and courageous. Do not fear or be in dread of them, for it is the Lord your God who goes with you. He will not leave you or forsake you." (ESV)

A special thanks to my Heavenly Father, who loves me just the way I am. I am forever thankful that I am His chosen daughter, even with all my beautiful mess! God has never counted me out, but instead, found me worthy to be used so that I could share this timely message about Him: The Great I AM, and our magnificent MESSIAH. I know that I could not have done this without Him, my loving Abba. THANK YOU, ABBA!

Dedication

To My Heavenly Father,

Thank you for giving me the opportunity to write this book, *In Heaven's Eyes*. I could not have done this without you, Abba, and I thank you for giving me the courage. You know exactly who will read this book, and I pray it will touch their lives as it has touched mine. Thank you!

To My Beautiful Family,

I wanted to take a moment to say thank you for your support, encouragement, and prayers. I could not have done this without your help: from wording, providing wisdom, suggestions on which photo to use, and the cover of the book. Always remember that you are Unique and a Beautiful MESS! You are loved!

To My Sisters in Christ,

You know who you are! Thank you for your prayers and for being my cheerleaders. Thank you, SISTAHS for being my #1 Fan.

Acknowledgements

To my hubby, Wawa, who loves me just the way I am as well as with my baggage of different shapes and sizes. He stood by my side even when I needed a whole lotta Coffee and Jesus. He stuck with me through the good, the bad and the ugly. Thank you for loving this crazy woman. I don't know who is crazier, you or me? Nevertheless, I love you!

To my dear children, I am so proud of all of you. God used you in every step of the way. He gave you skills and you used them well. I know I may have embarrassed you, but there is never a dull moment with moi. I am excited to see what God has planned for you in the future. I want to say thank you for being YOU. You are wonderfully made by the great Creator.

To my friends and family, thank you for your support and encouragement. You were there when I needed you in prayer, in writing, in laughter with tears streaming from your eyes, playing a game of Skip-bo, dancing to the Christmas music, watching Hallmark movies or HGTV shows, celebrating the special occasions or just simply sitting and drinking a cup of tea or more likely coffee. Each one of you is special in my heart in many different ways, and it is impossible to list everything and everyone. But what I can say is a great big Thank you!

A special thank you to Prosperity Publishing Company for believing in me and encouraging me with the process of writing this personal story! You answered all of my questions and concerns, and I loved the fact that we always started our discussions with prayer. A few people recommended that I write a book about my life, but I chickened out. Nonetheless, God said, “Daughter, you are not running away from me!” and that’s when He brought the wonderful team of Prosperity Publishing Company to my attention and I finally said yes to this humble opportunity. God knew exactly what He was doing, and I thank HIM for my obedience, and I thank YOU for being the great example of our Heavenly Father.

Chapter 1

In the Beginning

Picture this scene with me. The room in the scene was blurry yet some details seemed so vivid. There were green leather chairs that looked like they came from the period of 1970's and the walls were covered with wooden panels. A large cardboard box stood next to one of the green leather chairs, and it was filled with girl toys such as stuffed animals, doll house, and games. Also, someone parked a pink bicycle next to that cardboard box. On the other side of the room, it, too, had another set of green leather chairs. In one of those chairs, a beautiful young woman who was in her 20's occupied it. She had long black hair which had barrettes that pulled some hair up to the side. Her lap had something on it - a little girl who desperately held onto her. Her little eyes captured a man who sat in the chair next to that cardboard box. That man looked incredibly sad and had his head somewhat down. Still, she saw enough to see that he had brown eyes which matched his dark brown hair, and a mustache above his frowning lips. Just then he lifted his head up a bit to look at the little girl. He did not speak a word then brought his head back down. Then the scene began all over again which whooshed us back to that lady with hair barrette, to the cardboard box, to the little girl, and then back to the man. The scene played repeatedly. Was it a dream? Or was it a piece of real memories? Why did I always remember that part? Who was that man? What had happened? I did not know and went on with my life with no answers.

During the cold month of February in 1980, there was warm joy in my family enough to melt the snow in New England, Massachusetts. My mother, Betty, held her newborn in her arms. Thrilled that she finally had a baby girl, she was surrounded by her sons along with my dad, Miguel. You could sense happiness and excitement in the air! Her sons, Richard and Patrick, were already years older; in fact, between Patrick and I, our ages were 9 years apart! Richard was the oldest with blonde hair, and Patrick was the second oldest with brown hair. Betty had always wanted a girl, and she was beyond happy since her dream came to realization after 9 long years! In that time of her life, she had a best friend, Martha, who was like family to her. Martha already had kids, and just like Betty, she, too, had a girl and two boys! She brought her children, Sandra, Dylan, and Aiden with her to visit Betty and her newborn.

Sandra was the oldest and beautiful. Dylan was the second oldest. He always had a great heart for his loved ones, but he was also a troublemaker. Lastly, as for Aiden, he always loved to sit in any rocking chair with headphones on to jam himself to the music. It seems to me that when Aiden sat in the rocking chair, it always soothed his soul. Betty's and Martha's families became one tight knit family. Martha and Betty looked nothing alike. Martha was a short and skinny lady with short hair while Betty was tall and big. Martha often rode on my mother's back to go to the small Portuguese shop. Betty's personality was strong, and no one would dare to mess with her. On the outside, she gave off an aura of sweetness, was known as the life of the party, and had a sense of humor. She loved to make people laugh; even to the point where people could not help but pee in their pants! If you were with her, you might as well carry a Depend on you just in case! However, whenever anyone messes with those close to her, I would suggest you stay as far away as you can from her; going to California would be a suitable place to go if you live on the east coast. She was very protective of those close to her.

To further the closeness within the family, Betty became Aiden's godmother. At one point, she celebrated his first Communion and helped him cut his cake. She wore a navy-blue suit dress with white blouse, had her hair all curled back, and eyelids painted with sky blue eye shadow. Aiden proudly wore a navy-blue suit as well. They were peas in a pod with matching color tones.

Martha's daughter, Sandra, became a large part of my life. She always babysat me, or she really had no choice since I always followed her everywhere. She shared some stories about how I had "ruined" her life! One of my favorite stories involved the time when she took a nap one day. I walked into her room and decided to play with her lipsticks. On top of that, I thought I would treat my favorite babysitter to a drawing. A drawing drawn by lipsticks, and it was not on paper. It was directly on her television screen!!! Yes, you read it! I blessed her television with art! It is safe to say she really woke up after that and did not think twice about taking a nap again. Our families loved to get together so much to party and jam to the music. Oh, Christmas time was our all-time favorite holiday!

The happiness did not last long. When I was 2 years old, my mother knew she was sick, and death would soon take over her life. What about her children? That became her priority to talk with Sandra. Sandra had always looked upon Betty as her second mother besides her mother, Martha. Betty said, "Sandra, I know you love my children very much. Can you please take them under your wings?" All Sandra could do was to nod her head with sadness, and at that time, she was a young, beautiful 19- year-old lady. That is such a huge responsibility at that age! I admit I do not think that would be something I would have done if I found myself in that situation. I would rather travel and explore the world without the responsibility of someone else's toddler on my agenda. My mother, at the age of thirty-five, had passed away a month before my third birthday.

I went to live with Martha's family. Martha's daughter, Sandra, had officially adopted me. Not only did Sandra adopt me, but she also tried to adopt my two brothers as well to keep my family together. Unfortunately, the court would not grant them to her due to their closeness in age. Remember Sandra was only 19 years old. My oldest brother, Richard, was already 15, and Patrick my younger brother, was 11. Tragically, Richard was not ablet to handle our mom's passing and got involved with drugs that led to his death from overdose. Patrick ended up in a foster home.

Do not forget that Sandra's mother was my mother 's best friend! That made her my Grandma after Sandra adopted me! Through Grandma, she shared several stories about my birth mother. To this day, I only have one photo of her. In that photo, my mother held me in her arms, and I was only two years old. I had earrings on, and only two bottom teeth that poked through. We looked peaceful and happy. I think that we do look alike with the eyes and the nose. They always told me that I reminded them of Betty because of my sense of humor. I did not know what else we had in common. I had always wondered why my mother named me Kimberly. Was it to rhyme with her name-Betty- Kimmy!? I guess that would be one of the questions I would ask her when I get to heaven.

I am blessed to have my adoption letter that explained how my life had changed, and it helped me understand why some things happened. Here is my adoption letter. It was typed out to me on pastel pink papers in exact words with changes to names due to privacy:

> "You were born on February 9th, 1980, in Charlton Memorial hospital to your birth dad, Miguel, and your birth mom, Betty. You were your mom's third baby and first girl. She was really excited and showed all her friends her beautiful baby, Kimberly. Your mom, Sandra, who takes care of you, was a very good friend of your birth mom and would visit often. You and Sandra liked each other a lot and your birth mom would let Sandra babysit with you.
>
> Your mom's sons, Patrick and Richard, your brothers, also lived with you. They remember when you were as little as a doll and could only cry to get what you needed.
>
> Your birth mom and dad didn't get along and decided not to live together. Your

birth mom and dad decided you should grow up with your brothers. However, when you were 2 3/4 years old, your birth mom died after a long illness. She wished she could live to raise her children, but her body was too ill. Just before she died, when she was in the hospital, she asked her friend, Sandra, to care for you. She told Sandra, “I know that you will love my Kimberly as much as I do. Take good care of her. “I will”, said your mom, Sandra. And Sandra took you home too. She called your social worker, Joe, who talked to the Judge. The Judge said, “If Mrs. Betty and you feel that Kim will be safe and loved by Mrs. Sandra, I give you custody.”

That is how you came to have a birth mom, a mom who takes care of you, and a legal parent - Department of Social Services. When you were three years old, your mom, Sandra, noticed that you did not hear well. The doctor said that the fluid in your ears hurt them and you needed an operation.

The doctor put tiny tubes into your ears to help the fluid get out. This helped a little, but the tubes fell out and this time the fluid hurt your ears.

When little girls can't hear they can't learn to speak well. They go to special schools where they learn to speak with other people using American Sign Language. Your teachers at Regional Educational Assessment & Diagnostic Services (R.E.A.D.S) School have helped you learn this special language. When you learn all you can at R.E.A.D.S., you'll graduate to another school where you'll learn more about the world you live in.

Your Mommy Sandra and her husband Joseph's son, Joey, was born when you were four. Mommy remembers how you and she would touch her belly where Joey was growing, when he kicked. You and Mommy could tell Joey was a strong baby and soon he was big enough to leave Mommy's belly. Mommy went to the hospital and came home with your brother, Joey.

Your social worker, Joe, finally found your birth Dad in Providence, Rhode Island when you were four years old. Your dad said, "I want to visit with my daughter, Kimberly. He wanted you to live with him, but it was very hard for your daddy to care for you because in Puerto Rico, daddies don't learn how to take care of little girls. As much as your daddy loved you, he couldn't learn how to care for you. You and Mommy would go to Joe's office and visit your birth dad, Miguel.

When you were five years old, Joe asked Ann, the adoption worker, to meet you and your family. As you all love each other and want to grow up together, Ann will go to court and the Judge will give your mom, Sandra, permission to raise you until you are old enough to be on your own.This permission is called adoption. You were adopted on 4-6-87 and changed yourname to your mom's maiden name, S____."

My eyes have read those pink adoption papers from my adoption file repeatedly. It was not till last year when I finally took more notice between words and all. The whole time I thought I was already adopted at the age of three. The fact was I lived with Mommy Sandra for almost four years before my adoption became official and I became Sandra's adopted daughter. I found it interesting that the social worker wrote this type of straightforward letter for a girl who was almost 3 years old. I often wonder what the letter would say if she instead had to write to a teenager or even to an adult. Still, I am thankful the social worker took the time to write details, and it was all I had in my life. Better than none.

Chapter 2

Sweet Memories

Life became almost normal as I adjusted to new life with Mommy and Grandma. I was too young to understand the concept of difference between biological and adoption. I would not remember my birth mother if I did not have that only photo of us hung up on my bedroom wall. Thankfully, I grew to know more about my birth mother through Grandma who took the time to share details about her. There was another woman who was especially important in my life who I loved very dearly. She was called Vavó which is a Portuguese word for grandmother. She was Martha's mother and Sandra's grandmother. She did not speak any English. I wonder if she ever met my mother. I would assume so if Betty and Grandma were besties.

Vavó was a short, strong, and loving woman. Out of all the members in my family, she was the only one with short curly red hair! I wondered if she dyed it. She liked to wear simple clothing. Whenever she had important appointments, she always wore a black skirt with a yellow button-up short sleeve shirt, fancied up her hair, and carried a black leather purse on her right arm.

On all the other days when she did not have important appointments, she wore a smock with a pocket on each side to store her key and handkerchief. Nothing went to waste by her being frugal especially with water and electricity. There was no such thing as running a bath water or using a washing machine for small stuff such as socks. I remember she made me wash white socks by hand in a brown plastic bin then hang them to dry. She refused to use the vacuum cleaner. If you have a pet bird, let me be the first one to tell you… bless you, child! We used to have a parrot as a pet, and that colorful bird usually made a huge mess. The bird seeds often found its way out of the cage and ended up all over the orange carpet in the living room. Vavó made me get down on my knees to pick them up piece by piece until there were none on the carpet. I did so in obedience. Wouldn't it be a whole lot easier if we just used the vacuum cleaner? But no, not my Vavó! She cared more about our environment and liked to be economical especially with the electric bills. I agree with her on being considerate of the environment, but not to the extreme of being without a vacuum cleaner!

My other favorite memory was that she taught me how to sew by hand. I do not know how I did it with limited English speaking. I learned best through hands-on experience, and her teaching was very visual. She showed me step by step how to sew by hand, and thanks to her, I still sew to this day. Whenever there is a hole in my sock, it reminds me of Vavó. I remember whenever I went to vist her, I could tell if she was busy with sewing when I walked into her house. I felt the vibration through the floor when she used her old vintage sewing machine. I loved the feeling of the "sound" that vibrated through my little feet. Crocheting was another skill I had learned from Vavó. I crocheted many blankets for my own kids.

Vavó's cooking skills were amazing! I wish she taught me how to cook some of my favorite Portuguese dishes, but she always kicked us out of the kitchen as if her Portugese recipes were classified! I try to cook those dishes close enough to her recipes, but they are not the same still. She did teach me the most delicious dish we could have for breakfast or lunch. That was a grilled cheese sandwhich dipped in a cup of coffee. Yup, you did read this correctly! I did say COFFEE, that was the best part of the meal! Let the grilled cheese soak up the coffee then let it squish in your mouth. Yum, Yum, YUM! Even in the hot humid summer, we had that! Whereas during the winter, Vavó always had vanilla ice cream even if there was s snowstorm in New England. Another mouthwatering dish I had learned from Vavó was how to make a cantaloupe sandwich. She sliced the cantaloupe and placed the slices on white bread like lunch meat. That is it. I found myself on the memory lane about that dish many years later and decided to make it to see if my taste buds had changed or if Vavó was crazy. To my surprise it is still tasty and juicy! I even convinced one of my girlfriends who lived in Florida last summer to give it a try. She looked at me like I was out of my mind, but she did try it. I applaud her for her boldness to try it. Let's say she will not eat it again. That is understandable and fine, too. At least she tried it. I challengeyou to try it, too. You may like it!

We all have our own quirks. Vavó had one. I some- times wanted to help with putting groceries away. Vavó got upset with me if I held a gallon of milk close to my chest because she had the fear that if we did that, we would be liable to have a heart attack!

When she was not busy with sewing and cooking, we spent precious time together on her crochet blanket covered couch to watch a classic show called The Three Stooges. I remember the wall behind the couch had a vintage religious Jesus and His flock of Sheep velvet wall tapestry. The funny show always made Vavó laugh so hard, and she often blurted out, "meu Deus" (Oh my God) or "Maluco" (Lunatic). It was easy to laugh along with her! Think about it - she did not speak any English, and at the time, the television did not have the closed caption which functioned as subtitles that I could read the words of what actors said in the show. The show had plenty of comedic actions, and that was enough for us to enjoy the show. That reminds me of a popular saying, "Actions speak louder than words." So, I give the kudos to the Stooges' ability to make us laugh hilariously!

Every summer, Vavó took me out to her garden. Her garden had a variety of vegetables and fruits such as corn, cucumbers, and tomatoes of various kinds such as cherry and tomatillo. She even had a grape vineyard! Remember we lived in the city! It was not set up as an ordinary yard that you usually see in the country with rows and rows of grapevines. In the backyard, the yard already had a metal link fence all around. Inside that yard, the grapevines were set up among the metal crated pipes that were wide and high enough for us to go under the vines. Nothing was impossible with Vavó. We were able to pick the grapes off the vines when we stood under the pipes. Under the vines, there was a red picnic table for us to sit on to enjoy the delicious plum grapes. When we picked the grapes from the vines, we were not allowed to wash them. I wanted to since there were some spider webs on them, but Vavó said that we would insult Jesus if we washed them off. Of course, I rinsed them off when she did not look. Sorry, Vavó! I strongly believe that Jesus did forgive me for that and my other sins. The best part about Vavó's grapes - they were free!

I must share my sweet Christmas memories about Vavó and her kindness. At Christmas time, Vavó always draped her coffee table with a plastic table cover that had a design of red poinsettia. On the table, there was a sectional platter that was filled with cheese curls, potato chips, unsalted peanuts, wrapped butterscotch candies, and Hershey's Kisses.

She bought specific Hershey's Kisses in original silver foil wrappers; not the red and green foil wrappers that came out in the Christmas season. There also were grown-up drinks such as whiskey and beer. Orange sodas were available for the kids. Her door was always open for any visitors because she enjoyed having company. She was never alone during the holiday.

One of the things that I learned from Vavó about eating the Hershey Kisses was to slow down and not to chew it but to let it take the time to melt in your mouth. She demonstrated how I was supposed to eat the Kisses. Now that I look back, I can understand what Vavó wanted to tell me. She wanted me to not rush into things, take a step back, and enjoy every little thing. Yes, even sucking on the chocolate kisses can do the trick. Even many years later, the Kisses find its way into my shopping cart during the Christmas holidays. It always makes me think of Vavó , and that sure does bring a smile to my face. My dear Vavó has gone home with the Lord a few years ago. I am so grateful that my best other half met her. Vavó taught me how to live wisely, how to host parties, how to care for our planet, how to enjoy simple things, and how to clean the house.

Chapter 3

Says Who?

After Sandra adopted me, I called her Mommy. Mommy met a guy and got pregnant with a baby boy, Joey. He and I were 4 years apart in age. His father was never seen again and later, I learned that he was in a prison. I really do not know the whole story of what exactly went on even to this day. Some time had passed until one day my life had turned upside down by Mommy's decision. I recall the day when I played with my toys in the living room while Joey followed Grandma around the house. I looked up and saw Mommy walking into the living room with the look that she was upbeat and happy. While high on happiness, she announced, "Kimmy, come and meet your new daddy!" Confused by the surprise announcement, I looked at that man. He stood next to Mommy, and he was dressed in an Army uniform. Bewildered with his presence, I tried to understand how it was possible that he was now my daddy?!? I had never met him before. Eventually soon, he came and lived with us. Mommy got pregnant by him a few years later then again 2 years after and ended up with two boys, Henry and Andy. That made me ten years older than Andy.

Any little girl would love to play outside with friends, to play with toys, to join sports activities, and look forward to spring and summer break from school. But not this little girl, I hated the school breaks. Since a new daddy came into my life, I experienced fear and pain. All the fun and joy we had before disappeared when daddy became a part of our family. Every day during the school year, I had to hurry home to do my chores. I practically became a housekeeper. The chores involved cleaning throughout the house including all bedrooms, laundry, dishes, and some cooking. If I did not, then daddy became angry and in rage, he hit me. He also did many other terrible things to me. I did not understand why he chose to hurt me. He pushed me down the stairs, hit me with a metal pipe, and even used Andy's toy rubber baseball bat on me. I ended up with a black eye from that. When my teacher at the elementary school asked me what had happened, I did what I thought was best. I lied to the teacher and said that I fell and hit my face on the mailbox. The teacher called my home to verify my story of how I got the black eye. Of course, I got into trouble for lying to the teacher. I was in a no-win situation!

One of daddy's horrendous ways to discipline me involved my finger being bitten by him! After a bite, he sent me away to stand in a corner. In the meantime, while

I stood near the wall with my finger bledding and dripping down the wall. I had to wait until I was allowed to leave, then I was able to clean up the wall. I hated being in the corner. It was the scariest place to be for me since I am Deaf and could not hear or see behind me. I was afraid that daddy would come up behind me and hurt me again. His punishing ways became worse because his hits were hard enough to leave marks on my body, pulled my hair, put a bar of soap in my mouth, and more that felt like it would never end.

In first grade, I began to attend Confraternity of Christian Doctrine or CCD as it was often referred to as its abbreviation. CCD is a program to educate children in Catholic Church to prepare themselves for their first Holy Communion. Daddy drove me to the next town, Somerset, about 15 minutes from our home to drop me off there for CCD. Ironically, there was already CCD at a Catholic Church right across the street from our home. Instead, Mommy and daddy decided it was best for me to attend CCD in Somerset since it already had a class for Deaf students. During my time in CCD, I learned about the Ten Commandments of God and was bothered by the fourth Commandment as it says that you should "honor your father and your mother." I was only six years old when I started to pray every night, "God, if you are there, please send me to a different family." I did not understand why in the world I must obey my parents when daddy hurt me? I thought I did everything that I was supposed to do - get up in the morning, go to school, make good grades, go home, clean the house, cook dinner, take care of my brothers, never talk back, always listen to parents, and so on. So, why should I obey? What would I get out of this? Is there any reward? A free drink from Starbucks? Sure, I will take some more abuse. Seriously? It was always hard for me to walk in the class and not feel comfortable to pull my CCD teacher aside to ask her questions. It had always been between me and God, if He was listening to me somewhere in heaven, I sure hoped He would answer soon.

Over time, the teachers began to notice my battered body and questioned me about it. Of course, I did what I knew for my safety, I lied about it again. I knew if I had told the truth, I would only see more of daddy's anger. The social workers had come in and out of my life many times. They constantly asked me questions that I could not answer truthfully because daddy liked to stand or sit behind them and give me a straight look that came with a warning that he would be prepared to hurt me again. His look became a norm for me to know to stay silent or else.

During fifth grade, I was really depressed and unhappy. I did not know what to do or even think. So, during recess time, I wrote "I want to die!" with chalk on the brick wall of Henry B. Burkland Elementary School. I felt there was no point in keep living when I kept on getting hurt by daddy. I hated him so much.

I did not feel or think I was beautiful either. You should see my old school pictures. People teased me for my look. Some said I looked like a boy. On top of that, one of my favorite teachers unbelievably made a hurtful comment whenever I entered into her classroom, "Sesame Street brought you a letter I" to reflect my appearance as a skinny girl with my afro hairstyle that looks like a lowercase letter of I. It was hard to be mad at her since she was one of my favorite teachers. She was great at storytelling and drawings. Still, it pained me to get that kind of treatment from her at school and tolerated the abuses at home at the same time. How would she even know that? Nothing felt right anymore. I did not know what I thought when I wrote my feelings on the wall. I did not think about the possibility of getting caught.

Well, on that same day, I was asked to stay after school. I remember when I walked down the school hallway with my teacher and counselor and saw Mommy, daddy, and Grandma, that was when I realized I was in huge trouble! Together, we all walked down the hallway into another room. Counselor asked me all kinds of questions, and my family just sat there as observers. I answered whatever sounded good to daddy. As usual, he gave me the threatening look to keep my mouth shut and not to tell anyone the truth. So again, here I made up stories such as that I did not have any friends and was lonely. Sadly, the truth was I did have plenty of friends but could not bring myself to tell them what really happened behind the closed doors at home. After the conference, the counselor ordered that I was to attend a mental health hospital for more checkups. Thankfully, I was able to attend school the next day.

On September 15th, 1989, we moved out of the city and moved to Dighton, MA. Before the big move, we lived in a building that housed five apartments in Fall River. My Grandma, Vavó, uncle, family friends and us all lived in that building. We all shared the laundry room in the basement. I enjoyed the visit to Vavó's apartment, and the best part, the walk was just a few steps away. The move to a new home was a tremendous change. It was a red, one level single family house with black shutters. It had an attic and basement. To get to the basement, we had to go out of the house and go around to the back. The basement floor was all gravel. We stored mostly tools, lawnmower, and dog food there. Our black lab dogs, Blackie and Lucky, stayed outside in their own dog houses with a chain fence. They were not even allowed to go in the house except for our fancy dog, she was a Chow-Chow. The yard was huge compared to the city's which had no grass yard and was covered in cement. We even got blueberries growing in the backyard. Our house was situated near the Taunton River on the left side of the yard. There was a curved driveway with a big tree in the middle of the driveway. Eventually, daddy added a tire swing to the tree. Not only that, he added white and red stepping stones that lead up into the middle of the house. We rarely used that door. I think it was there for decoration.

Our red house on a half-acre land had three bedrooms and one full bathroom near the boatyard upon the river. Because of the location of our house at the very end of the road, it felt a lot quieter. At that time when you looked at the house from the street, there were two entries, one on the left and one on right in the middle of the house. I wonder if the left side of the house was added on later. Only God knows. On the left side of the house, there was a wooden deck that was used as the main entry as it was closer to the curved driveway. When we walked into the house from the deck, we found ourselves in the formal dining room. Then on your right, there was a step up that led us to the tiny kitchen. In the kitchen on the left side there was a refrigerator, sink with countertop, and stove in the right corner. The washer and dryer set up there as well. Our kitchen table was right in the middle of the kitchen. Outside of the kitchen, there was a narrow hallway that led straight to my parents' bedroom and a bathroom was on your left.

To the right of the kitchen was the living room. My brothers' bedroom was on the right side of the kitchen, and my bedroom was on the left. All three of my brothers had to share one tiny bedroom. In their room, there was a bunk bed and a red metal toddler bed. Their toys were shoved underneath beds to save space, and they had one tall dresser. I remembered daddy was so proud to show me my room because my parents worked hard to remodel it. Carpet was pink! I had a white canopy bed with pink ruffled bed sheets, and walls covered with white wallpaper with tiny pink flowers. My sliding closet doors doubled as mirrors so that I could stand in front of it and model myself. I had an old- fashioned wooden TV that sat on the floor. Remember that big heavy bulky TV? I absolutely loved that TV because it had a closed caption box on it, that meant I could understand and enjoy shows! The most favorite room of the house was my bedroom because it was the only place where I felt most safe.

The only thing that had not changed was daddy's expectations of me. I still had to take care of housekeeping, and my brother, Joey, was now ordered to join me to the housekeeping responsibilities. I noticed that Joey and I were the only ones who got hurt by daddy more than the younger brothers. Joey was always my ears while I was always his eyes. We watched out for each other. We were so close and had our own hand signs for communication. He alerted me of dangers. His heart was caring and compassionate for people around him.

I would never forget the time when Joey came home from school all happy. I asked him what was up. He told me that he liked one girl from school, and he showed me his first-grade class picture. She was cute and pretty in her red and white dress all dolled up for the photo shoot. I cheered him on and told him, “Aww, that was so cute!” daddy heard my cheers and wanted to know what the fuss was all about. Joey told him and proudly showed him the photo. Then daddy said something that I still to this day would never forget. He had the nerves to tell Joey, “Milk and chocolate do not go together.” I was shocked that he would say the meanest thing! I disagreed! Oreos and milk taste so delicious together. I do not know what this crazy man thought! When I saw the look on my brother, Joey’s face was in disbelief. In a single moment, he went from being happy to being heartbroken. Since that moment, I never heard him talk about liking anyone again. I do not blame him. Daddy was never kind to us. Joey was only in first grade, and like me, he learned to keep his mouth shut. He learned to be careful with what he chose to share with family. Whatever happened to feeling safe and being ourselves, carefree without walking on stepping stones in our own home?

The life in Dighton had become darker and darker. I saw things that I should not have ever seen - to see my parents do drugs such as cocaine and marijuana. Daddy never smoked cigarettes, but my baby brother, Andy, who was about 3 years-old did not know any difference. There was one incident when Andy went to our parents’ bedroom and immediately ran out to my room to tell me, “Mimi, daddy’s smoking!” Of course, who came behind Andy? You guessed it right. Daddy told him to shut up. Poor Andy! He was just a toddler and completely innocent. My thoughts wanted to think out loud, "Um, excuse me. Daddy, I may be Deaf, but I am not blind. I saw some things, too. On top of that, I could literally smell marijuana on you!" This did not make any sense for daddy to chew Andy out for being truthful of what he saw. After that incident, Andy just wanted to sit right next to me. Sadly, he did not feel safe with his own daddy.

There were times where both Mommy and daddy fought to the point where he hit her hard enough to break her nose and knee. During those argumentative times, there were times Joey just had enough and wanted to throw the brick to end their argument and tried to protect our Mommy. I applaud his bravery. He retreated to his room and tried to cover his ears to block out the sounds. I felt bad for him because I am sure he heard a lot more than I did.

Another frightful tragedy that I cannot forget was when Mommy and daddy fought each other outside near the steps to the deck. Our dog, Blackie, tried to protect Mommy when daddy hurt Mommy. Blackie stepped in and bit daddy. In daddy's mind, our dog attacked him. That made daddy more furious. Furious enough to drag Blackie by his collar and brought him behind the pool to kill him with a baseball bat!!! He murdered our dog! I was livid at him. That heartless man had the nerve to walk up to me with a smile on his face and claimed that Blackie had rabies. Baloney!!!

The truth was simple - daddy murdered our dog. All Blackie did was to try to protect my Mommy. Blackie was a very loving and loyal dog. Even a dog could tell that daddy was up to no good. I do not know if any of my brothers saw what I saw that day, and I prayed that they did not. That traumatic moment is forever stuck in my memory and I wish I never had seen that. Our home was not a safe place to be at. My favorite time of the day was at night because that is when I said my same prayer that I have said since I was 6 years old.

Two celebrations, Father 's Day and Veteran's Day, were not easy for me and Joey. Our two younger brothers were so young to remember or understand what went on around them. During the school years, my teachers organized activities that involved us to make gifts for both Mother 's Day and Father 's Day. Once for a Father's Day gift, we were to make a huge chocolate chip cookie. The students worked together to mix all the ingredients together then bake them. After the cookies cooled off, we wrote “Happy Father 's Day” on the cookies with the white icing. Afterwards, we went home with cookies to give to our fathers. Well, in my case, the ride home was long from school, and I was already hungry. I decided then to eat the gift! The cookie tasted really good, and I had no regrets either. I hated Father 's Day and thought there was no way in the world daddy deserved a gift of any kind! Well, it looks like God had other plans.

Our Mommy told us to stand in the living room so that we could give daddy a gift that Mommy got him. We stood and let her do her thing. Joey and I saw what she got him. A wooden picture frame with engraved words, "Anyone can be a father, but it takes someone special to be a Dad." Joey and I were in disgust and did not agree with the quotation. Really, this dude was even nowhere close to being SPECIAL, and he never will be our "Dad." I wanted to throw up. If I was to be honest, I was incredibly grateful that we were not even blood relatives. Though, I kind of felt bad for the younger brothers. Please forgive me Lord for saying this.

As for Veteran's Day, I was not sure if all the people who wore uniforms hurt their own families at home as well. It was simply hard for me to see past that. A man in an Army uniform who was in service for our country was supposed to be honorable in his actions. How can Mommy bring him home and think he would be that type of man? Behind the closed door, he was nowhere a Hero and did not even for a minute earn the right to be called "daddy", with his abuses toward us. You cannot be a hero to our country if you cannot be a HERO in your own home behind the front door and inside those four walls. It does not matter what military branch you are in and wear its uniform, you may come off as a hero in public for your service. But the truth is a real HERO begins with your own family and be a great role model for your children, so that they could be great Heroes because of your example.

There's Hope

In my middle school years, I attended Raynham Jr. High School. I was a bit excited for the new chapter as a teenager. I thought it was cool that the school had lockers, had home economics class that taught students how to cook meals, sewing, and even care for a "baby" egg. Oy, I remembered those good ole days. I was so nervous as my home economics teacher called out each student's name to pair up with another student. We had to work with a student to take turns to care for our "baby" and had to find out what was wrong with the baby. We had to figure out what type of diseases or disabilities that our "baby" may have been born with. Our "baby" had spina bifida. Many years later, I cannot believe that I still remember this.

Another favorite memory I had was the time all the sixth graders studied the history of the 1950-60's era and watched a movie called *Grease* with John Travolta and Olivia Newton-John in it. Then some of us performed songs from *Grease* or any song from the 1960's era. I loved to watch MTV or VH-1 videos on TV. From those shows, I tried to copy their dance movements. I really wanted to be a performer. By the grace of God, I did a performance on a song called *Lipstick on Your Collar* by Connie Francis. Oh, wait! Let me tell you a short story about how I ended up doing that song.

My Mommy used to take me out for karaoke nights. It was so cool just the two of us. My aunties and cousins joined us there at the karaoke bar. Kids had soda pops while the grownups drank beer. At one time, it was Mommy's turn to sing. She sang the *Lipstick on Your Collar,* and I read the lyrics as the words scrolled up on the karaoke screen. I loved the beats and the oldies mood. I loved it so much that I wanted to do this song for the 1960's show at my school.

To be prepared for my part in the show, I met with a speech therapist. Usually, the therapist came over to my classroom to take me out of the class for our once-a- week sessions. I used to hate being pulled out of my classroom to meet with the speech therapist. But for the show, I was happy to get all her help. I had to practice and memorize the lyrics. I had brought in the cassette tape that had a recording of Mommy's singing that song from the karaoke night. Much later I learned that Mommy was furious and embarrassed that I shared the tape. To my Deaf ears, the tape sounded so beautiful. It reminded me how much fun Mommy had that night. I did not know that the sound was totally different from what my Deaf ears heard. For the hearing folks, they heard how intoxicated Mommy sounded on the tape. Oops! Sorry, Mommy! No wonder why my speech therapist looked at me in a funny and puzzling way. She tried to listen to the tape repeatedly to catch the words Mommy sang with no success. We then had to buy a new cassette tape of the original singer.

On the show day, I had a blast! For my showcase, I needed two background actors to act like my boyfriend who was with another lady. When I asked one of the basketball players at junior high school, he turned it down. I found a different guy who accepted the small part. My performance caused the students to shout and chant to root us on. I may be Deaf, but I sure can perform! I loved being a performer, and music had that calming effect on my soul. After we finished the performance, that basketball player approached me and said, “You did a great job, and I am sorry I did not perform with you when I should have.” Yup! He should have! But then, I was already used to others’ rejections. Most teenagers or I should say, most hearing people, just did not know how to approach Deaf folks. We will not bite! You just need to have an open mind and a willing heart to learn from us.

Remember VHS tapes in those old days? My performance was recorded on a tape. I excitedly brought the tape back home to share with my parents. They did come to the show but arrived late and did not catch my part in the performance. We were in the living room to watch it. Mommy had this huge smile on her face and jammed to the music. Mommy shouted out to daddy, "Babe, come see this! Kimmy's performance." Daddy did not really care. He had no words for me. He came over and stood for a bit then left to do his thing. Mommy was proud of me. It was then that I realized that I was interested in trying out for cheerleading. It did not take very long for my parents to stomp that idea out. Their claim was that the drive to school was too long. In fact, the drive was only 25 minutes. I guess anything that took longer than 10 minutes was just too far. Perhaps my parents had other reasons. As a junior high school student, I wanted to try and explore many new things. It was not possible but to be at home to do chores and homework. Oh, the joy of being in Jr. High.

Growing up, I always had a sign language interpreter with me in several classes. I sat in the very front row; sometimes so close to the blackboard that I could touch it; especially when the class had so many students in the room. Interpreters usually sat across from me. When I began middle school, it was no different. I had a new interpreter, and I loved her! I called her Ms. Rosey because her cheeks were always red and her nose, too. She could pass as Santa Claus' wife. She was short, a bit round in body, and sported short gray hair. She always wore glasses with strings; so, when she took her glasses off, it rested on her chest. Without fail, she always carried a bag filled with goodies such as yarns, books, etc. to keep herself entertained when she was on a break from interpreting in classes or when students had to work quietly on their schoolwork. She always had funny stories to share with us. Boy, when she laughed, tears flowed from her eyes!

Every Friday, there was always a story time. I know it seemed strange for middle schoolers to have that. Story time probably was common for students in elementary school. Odd or not, I loved every minute of it. My teacher who specifically taught Deaf and Hard of Hearing students chose chapter books to read to us. I remember a book series called *The Boxcars Children* written by Shepard Bob. Ms. Rosey interpreted while our teacher read the book aloud. After a chapter or two, we had to answer some questions about it and write a brief summary of the story. This was a fantastic way to promote and expand our English writing skills since English is considered a second language whereas American Sign Language was our first language. I know back in the time we used to moan and whine about writing. But it was the best investment of our time, and it paid off in the long run. Thank you to that teacher, you know who you are.

There were so many sweet moments at that school. I want to share one that touched my heart the most. One day when I headed for lunch, I realized I forgot something and had to return to the classroom to get it. When I walked back into the classroom, I noticed my teacher and Ms. Rosey had their heads down. They were to have lunch together at a table, but they did not eat when I saw them.

They bowed their heads down to pray! I snuck out before they caught me. I am not sure if they heard me. That memory of them praying etched in my mind forever. It was awesome to see them praying together. Only God knew their prayers at that time.

Ms. Rosey asked if I would like to attend church with her. I thought that it was nice of her to ask me, and at the same time, I thought anywhere but home would be great. I told Ms. Rosey, "Yes, I would love to." Of course, she had to call Mommy to make plans. One Sunday morning, Ms. Rosey picked me up and drove us to Taunton Assembly of God church. I was with her for one of the little kids' Sunday school classes. Ms. Rosey was a volunteer to teach the children a bible lesson. I cannot remember which lesson that was, but I clearly remember I was in awe of her lesson and her interaction with the little boys and girls. Afterwards, we went to the church service. The space was not big; just enough to give off the warm cozy feeling. Ms. Rosey sat in the front of the pew to interpret the sermon. The pastor made an announcement and welcomed the visitors. He asked for those who were guests to please stand up and I did. Then the church began to play worship songs.

I remember clearly there was one song that got people in the sanctuary to stand up shouting and singing. While they jumped up and down, they all waved their white handkerchief in the air. I just looked around and could not believe what my eyes saw. They smiled and praised God with this line out of their mouths, “I got the Joy Joy Joy JOY down in my heart to stay!!” I remember that one line. There was something so powerful and so moving about the service. I had never seen such pure happiness, peace, and joy on people’s faces before. I did not know if it was a culture shock or something. Whatever I just witnessed sure moved me! While the offering dish had been passed around in the sanctuary, there was a song playing. As I watched Ms. Rosey interpret the song, something moved in my heart, and I felt overwhelmed in my mind. Before I knew it, tears flowed down my face as I continued to see the words of Sandi Patti’s song, In Heaven’s Eyes:

“In heaven’s eyes, there are no losers

In heaven’s eyes, there is no hopeless cause

There’s only people like you with feelings like me

And we’re amazed by the grace we can find

We can find In heaven’s eyes”

I sobbed yet felt very hopeful. I was grateful to know that God does love me. To believe that I was indeed worthy! He does hear my cries, my prayers, my anger, and my EVERYTHING. I was sure that God was heartbroken when He saw daddy hurt me and others in the family. This song gave me new hope when I thought I was hopeless and wanted to end my life a few years back. This song gave me more strength to go on and to try to keep my head up. Now I realized that I was not alone anymore since I have Jesus and Ms. Rosey. I am forever thankful that Ms. Rosey took some of her time on that one Sunday morning to drive over to another town to pick this broken little girl up and to help her to hear His Truth. I was sure Ms. Rosey had no idea what went on in my life. I was just a student at Jr. High school. This song may be old, but it has forever changed me. It still to this day is one of my favorite songs. So, for those who may feel down or hopeless, seek this song out. Listen, read, and study the words. Keep them close to your heart because YOU indeed are WORTHY. Based on my own experience, I believe with all my heart that there is HOPE during the hopeless situations. Please do yourself a favor, do not lose HOPE and hold on to His Truth. Jesus indeed loves YOU. If He did not, He would not have sacrificed his life on the cross! He did that because you and I are WORTHY. He loves YOU. Yes, I am talking to you. Even YOU!

Fought a Good Battle

My first year in high school, I attended Bristol-Plymouth Regional Technical School. Let's go, Craftsman! Who would have thought a boy would play a significant role during my first year in high school? It led me to a whole new chapter of my life. How funny how it all began with this one boy. To understand the seriousness of the situation with daddy, the boy I liked was not a Portuguese. Daddy expected me to date a Portuguese guy or not date at all. Anyways, there was a boy I really liked, and he just happened to be Black. I knew not to bring him home or even mention anything about this young fella to anyone in the family. I knew better. Remember what had happened to my brother, Joey, in the previous chapter. How he endured daddy's harsh words about him, liking a Black girl.

It just so happened that my birthday was only a few days before Valentine's Day. In this case, a boy surprised me with overflowing gifts for both special days! Bless that boy's heart! In shock, I could only utter, "Thank you." I was not able to squeeze all the gifts into my high school skinny locker. I made the decision to put the gifts in my homeroom. Few days later, my teacher finally told me to please take my gifts out of the classroom. I really did not want to bring my gifts home to avoid my parents' reaction or risk the possibility that the boy may think I did not want them. I did not want to hurt his feelings. I was nervous about what my parents would say about these gifts. I prayed for God's help to give me the courage to bring my gifts home. Of course, Mommy saw my gifts and wanted to know everything about it. Her curiosity got the best of her, and she immediately wanted to have a mother/daughter talk which was exceedingly rare. I had to deal with Mommy's endless interrogation. I gave in and answered, "Some boy likes me." Short and simple answer! Who knew that would be enough to push daddy's anger over the cliff?

Remember I wrote earlier about being in the CCD class? The situation brought me back to my struggle as a Catholic and with two of the Ten Commandments. The first part was to honor your father and mother, and the second part was that you shall not lie. It threw me in a twist. I still could not apply my life to those two commandments - honor parents and do not lie. I compared my life a bit to Cinderella's story - I must do whatever daddy says or I will get whupped by daddy's anger. I wanted to tell the truth, and Mommy made it more difficult with her questions. She wanted to meet the boy. I responded that I do not know when and tried to stall for more time. Only if she knew why I did not want to say anything!

As the time passed, I felt increasingly uncomfortable that I kept a secret from Mommy. I prayed for God's guidance and waited until daddy left the house to do his errands. With daddy out of the house, I took it as an opportunity to tell Mommy the truth. I had to find a way to explain the reason I had not brought the boy to our house. I could not be straightforward with the reason; that it was because of his skin color. I was so afraid to spit it out right away. I looked around for a different way. We were in the living room, and it was filled with Mommy's favorite collection of Native American - Native Americans dolls, art, home decorations, and even her couch. The fabric of her couch had colors of orange, green, ivory, and black colors. When I finally had the courage, I told Mommy, "The reason why you have not met him was because…" then paused to raise my finger to point at the black on her couch. Her reaction initially shocked me. She smiled and said, "Oh, Kimmy, that is OK. Your grandfather was Black." I did not know that! That was the last thing I expected to come out of her mouth!

A little flashback to a few years ago, I was in my bedroom where it had that picture on the wall of my birth mother holding me when I was 2 years old. One of my cousins walked into my room just to see what I was up to then I noticed he stood silently with his eyes glued to that picture. I asked him what was wrong. He pointed to the picture and asked who these people were. I told him that it was me and my mother. He did not believe me at all and told me to stop with the jokes. I was surprised by his answer, and I told him again that it was my mother with me when I was 2 years old. He said, "No way! That does not look like her!" He pointed to my Mommy who sat in the living room. I realized then my cousin thought that the woman in the picture was my Mommy. He was right about one thing - Mommy and my birth mother do not look alike. It dawned on me that he just did not know that part of information about me. I explained, "That is my Mommy in the living room, but the one in the picture was my birth mother. I am adopted." He was shocked and said that he had no idea. I did have people tell me that Mommy and I looked alike. I guess that can happen when you grow up with the adopted family that you start to talk and behave like them and blend in easily.

Later that night after my cousin and others left, I found daddy and Mommy on the deck. daddy asked me why I told my cousin about that picture on the wall and asked if I did not love my Mommy. He told me that I hurt her feelings when I shared with others that I was adopted. So, since that experience, I had decided not to share with anybody about my life before my adoption. Perhaps I was the top secret in the family. I thought it was strange and did not make any sense.

If Mommy did not want me to tell people that she adopted me then why in the world did I have that photo up on my bedroom wall? In fact, I did not put that up there. I knew better than to touch the walls because daddy would kill me if I made holes in the wall. Since then, I kept my mouth shut and never brought up about my biological background again. There were times when I did ask Grandma about my family history. She either could only answer what she remembered or shared only superficial details.

Back to that time when Mommy spilled out about my biological grandfather being Black, I was so taken aback with that new information. Was he really? I was shocked and of course, confused. I wanted to know more and wanted to ask her a zillion questions. I knew best that I better not so I would not hurt her feelings with my desire to know more about my blood relatives. Still, I felt so much better after I told Mommy the reason, she could not meet this fella. There was no more secret, and it felt good to get it off my chest. My burden had been lifted, but I kid you not, that feeling only lasted for a moment.

After I told Mommy the reason why she had not met him, I went back to my chores. I was in the dining room to vacuum when daddy came home from his errands run and walked straight to his bedroom. He closed the door then before I knew it, he opened the door again. Mommy must have told him what had happened earlier. From where I stood in the dining room, I saw him open the doorand quickly walked up to me.

He hit the roof and screamed at me. Then he asked me if I had kissed a "N" word, and I told him I did. He punched and slapped me. Within a few minutes, that night turned into a nightmare. He could have ended my life, and I would not be here today. Daddy tortured me with whatever he could get his hands on such as metal pipe and even tool pliers to hit my knee. My body was like a raggedy doll to him. He dragged me across the floor to my bedroom and continued with his hits on me. Finally, he stopped. Wait, he was not done with me. He picked me up and threw me on my bed, then turned away. I found myself on my bed with my back facing the wall, and I watched my bedroom door to stay alert and be prepared in case he came back for more.

A few minutes later, the phone rang, and Mommy answered it. She came into my room, "Kimmy, your friend is on the phone." I thought to myself you got to be kidding me! I just got beaten up, and you wanted me to answer the phone?! I did so in obedience and took the phone off Mommy's hand. Back then, I was able to talk on the phone, but that did not mean that I understood everything 100% that was being said. When I answered the phone, it turned out that it was the Black fella that I liked - the very exact boy for whom I had gotten beat up. You know when the teenage boys get their voice all cracked up through puberty - well, he took that advantage to pretend he was a girl on the phone. So, when I got on the phone he asked, "Kimmy, are you OK? Something tells me I had to call you!" What I did not realize until later was that it was God the whole time, and He was there with me!

I answered him back, "I am fine." He changed back to a normal voice. What I did not know was that daddy was on the other phone line in his bedroom listening to our conversation. Daddy then told the boy nasty things, then he went back into my bedroom to hit me once again, and more. In my defense, I accidentally kicked him in between his legs, and God clothed me with His mighty strength to say these words, "The colors do not matter, what is inside matters!" My Mommy was on the phone with Vavó, and she was in pure shock that I had spoken back to daddy. She had the nerve to laugh and told Vavó what had just happened while he resumed his beatings. Daddy had to have the final word after he had hit me and screamed, "I wish you would get the 'beep' out of here!" That was when I knew exactly what I had to do. Thank you for giving me the opportunity to leave this storm.

The next day, I arrived at school and told my teacher that I refused to attend any of my classes until something that needed to be taken care of. The unmistakable evidence of suffering on my body had shown all my pains, and I was not even able to sit down since it was too painful. Again, with God's strength still clothed on me, I explained what had happened to my teacher. My teacher then called the social worker, and she came to the school right away. The social worker and I were placed into a different room for privacy along with an interpreter whose name was Maddy. The social worker asked me tons of questions, and I was forever grateful that Maddy was there with me during this process. I did not know what I would do without her, and she always had my back. I was furious and upset. My emotions were all over the place. I bluntly told the social worker that social workers were foolish. The whole time that the social workers had come in and out of my life to conduct checkups on my welfare, to ask endless questions, and to visit me at school during my childhood were futile. They assumed I was perfectly fine. Really? Look at me! Does this look anything close to fine? How in the world could they be so foolish and naïve to ask me all kinds of questions in front of that monster? And for that reason, I could not tell the whole truth.

This time for the very first time the social worker listened intently, and I did all the talking. We worked out a plan on what to do after I arrived home from school at the end of the day. The plan was that there would be a social worker there to speak with my mommy and wait for my arrival. I remember the ride on the bus on the way home felt like the time ticked so slowly. It felt like it took forever to get home that day. I was worried about what would happen when I arrived home. What if my parents were home, then what? I even tried to come up with a plan A, B, C, and so forth.

With such a relief, daddy was not home as he was still at work, and Mommy was not home either! I went straight inside the house and tried to do what I normally do daily. I did some chores. Well, I tried. It was indeed hard to stay focused on chores. I was so shaken up inside and looked out my bedroom window to see if my parents had arrived home. Finally, I saw Mommy pull up into the driveway then the social worker pulled up behind her. By now I knew what kind of mood Mommy could be in by her body language. She was furious. Apparently, the social worker had already spoken with her because Mommy came into my bedroom and said, “You don’t want to live here anymore?! Then here are the trash bags and get out of here!” I was surprised, shocked, felt hurt by her words, and did exactly that. I thought I did the right thing. I wanted that man out of the house, not me. I guess she had chosen him over me. So, I did what she told me to do, and that was to throw my clothes into my new baggage - aka trash bags. It took me a while to figure out what else to take with me, and I had no idea where I was going to be taken to next. I did not really pack much. As I packed, my Grandma showed up to give Mommy her support because Mommy cannot manage any crisis. What about me? They sat down at the kitchen table with the social worker.

My brother, Joey, now at the age of ten came home from school. He came into my room to tell me the highlight of his day and shared what he had learned something new from his music class. I put on my best smile and congratulated him. He beamed with a smile from ear to ear and left my room. I tried to stay strong, but I was dying inside. I went back to packing my bag. Few minutes later, Joey came back into my room and slowly closed my door behind him. His eyes glanced from me to my pile of clothes then asked, "Kimmy, why is Mommy crying? What is going on and what are you doing?" I stopped with my packing and told Joey to come closer. "Joey, I love you very much, and I want to let you know that I am moving." Joey was so upset and yelled, "Nooo!! Daddy will hit me worse now." He broke down and cried. I held him tighter and told him that he needed to be STRONG. He was not alone, and that I will be sure to be in touch. He nodded, wiped his tears, signed "I love you," and left the room. My heart broke in a million pieces. We always got each other 's back- he was my ears, and I was his eyes. I was scared for my boys - my brothers.

When I finally got out of my room and walked toward the kitchen, I saw my Grandma and Mommy seated at the kitchen table. I walked past them and heard Mommy say this to Grandma, "See! She did not even say goodbye!" I stopped on my way out, but the social worker gently put her hand on my back to urge me to keep on walking.

I do understand why the social worker did that. Often when parents say things to make a child feel guilty, the child might feel bad and change their mind with the decision to move out of their current home. It is for the best to move forward with the decision even when it is the hardest thing to do. It was very hard for me. I loved my family, but I did not like being hurt all the time. No more of being a punching bag for daddy. Enough was enough. As I walked out of the house, I remember I stood on the deck and looked to my right. Boys sat in the swings in the backyard, and I felt that God just stopped those moments long enough for me to look at them one last time before I left home. I got into the social worker's car and drove away. I did not know where I was going next for the long term; other than staying with my best friend, Y.B., for a few days until further notice.

I was grateful that my best friend, Y.B., and her mother allowed me to stay with them for a few days. I was at peace, yet I worried about my brothers and Mommy. I tried to focus on school, but it was a bit of a challenge. My social worker showed up at my best friend's place and told me that I needed to move to a different foster home. I was sad as I did not want to go; Y.B.'s momma hugged me and told me to be careful out there. I grabbed my bags and followed the social worker. I got into her car once again and had no idea where I was headed. I feared the unknown.

When I arrived, I met new foster parents, and they immediately told me their names. It did not matter because I forgot their names almost immediately. Either they were not important to me or did not impress me at all. You can tell if people care and show genuine compassion. They were a bit cold in their greeting. It was as if they ran a fast-food service. It is like they have several foster kids come and go in their house. I felt like I was a number to them. That was how I felt when I went into their home. They had two kids of their own - a daughter who was already in high school and a son who was about 5 years old. Besides me, they were already foster parents to two other Black teenage girls. One of the girls was my best friend, Y.B.'s cousin! I was a bit relieved that I knew at least one person in the house.

The foster girls showed me my room, and it turned out that they were my roommates. I tried to get settled in and then came down for dinner. The foster parents explained that I needed to start calling them "daddy" and "Mommy." There was no way I was going to call them that since they were practically strangers to me, and I had just arrived a few hours prior to dinner that night! Nah, I needed time before I could consider that. No, thank you. I just kept on calling them by their first names.

Either I was still in culture shock or struggled with the adjustment to this new home environment. Their boy was absolutely a wild kid. He ran around and screamed his head off while his sister did not care nor showed any respect. She swore here and there. I kid you not, their house was filthy. The kitchen sink was piled up with dirty dishes. It was just so different from what I was used to. These kids got plenty of freedom with no responsibilities. I was not used to this. Usually, I stayed on my bed. My room had a skylight which allowed me to see stars at nighttime. I had already missed a couple of days of school only because the foster parents did not want to drive me to school! My school that had a program for the Deaf was out of their district, and the driving time was an inconvenience to the foster parents' schedule. The transition started to make me doubt myself. I missed my friends and teachers. That doubt crept into my mind and had me feel I had probably made a huge mistake leaving my family. I cried several times and prayed to whoever would listen to me that I want to be anywhere else but here. This was not what I had pictured about the new family and fell asleep.

Days went by which seemed like weeks. It felt like forever in the world of the unknown. Then one afternoon, the foster dad said that I got a phone call and needed to come down to the kitchen. I went downstairs and picked up the phone. To my surprise it was from my middle school teacher! She said, "Hi Kim, just wanted to let you know that we have room for you if you want to come and live with us?" Simple and plain as that! I was thrilled and thought, "Anywhere but here. For sure!" The foster dad heard our conversation. I was so happy. It was one of the best gifts! I was beyond happy that I could live with someone that I already knew, and on top of it, that someone is who I can communicate with through sign language. Strangely, the foster dad was not happy with the fact that I was happy. I looked forward to moving out of this mad house. He literally asked me, “What? You are not happy living here?” Really?!? I do not get it. Why did people have to ask me this question? I just looked at him, shuddered my shoulders and went back up to my room to count down the days until my social worker came and picked me up from this mad house.

Chapter 6

A New Life

It was the day when the social worker came to pick me up from the previous madhouse. I only had two black trash bags of my things which were mostly clothes. I got into the car to meet with my new foster parents. I can still remember the moment when we pulled up into their driveway. I was comfortable enough to get out of the car and walk up the steps to their screen door. My teacher opened the door and hugged me. Then I met her husband. He reached out his hand for a handshake. For some reason, I felt peace and did not experience any fear as soon as I stepped into their home. I had never felt that before. Not once till that day. Instead of a handshake, I gave him a hug. My teacher showed me where my bedroom was and to my surprise, I became overwhelmed by the community's love and generosity. As soon as I walked into the room, I saw there were tons of gifts on top of my new bed! Their friends and family threw them a "teenager" shower! Here I was with only two black trash bags, and that changed when I came into this full of blessings. Of course, there were no dry eyes!

After the social worker got me settled in and left, three of us went shopping to get what I needed for the night. They wanted me to pick out a few things like bed sheets and a bathrobe. I can still clearly visualize what my bedding set looked like - a reversible sheet with one side of pink roses with green leaves print while the other side had pink and white stripes. I thought that was so cool! The color of my own new bathrobe was purple. Purple was and will always be my favorite color. Afterwards, we went to Pizza Hut for dinner, and it was a fantastic way to get to know each other. Since then, the foster parents became my Momma and Poppee. It sounded better and more hip.

There were many new things that I had to get used to, especially to what was expected at the kitchen table. The kitchen table was where everyone in the family gathered, said our grace, ate our meals together, and talked about our day. This was indeed different compared to when I lived with my adopted family. My dinner time experience with my adopted family was mostly just me and my brothers while my Mommy and daddy ate in the living room. I never had a family conversation with my parents. They did not even ask how our day was at school or anything like that. The new life with Momma and Poppee was a learning experience. I learned how to live. That was the best way of describing it. We all shared chores and worked together as a team. My momma had always come into my room to collect my clothes from the laundry basket.

I did not have to wash or fold the clothes but to put my clothes away. Talk about a whole load off my shoulder. After weekly chores, I had an allowance. Again, I did not have that growing up. Today I am aware that not every family has an allowance. Each family has different beliefs and expectations. I respect that. I was glad I had an allowance since it taught me money management and how to give as well.

There was another one of my favorite memories but not at that time when I was fourteen years old. Believe it or not, I had never learned how to use a fork and knife during the meals. It was even more challenging to cut chicken with the bones. My momma taught me how to cut the chicken. Oh, what a joy! There was one time when I struggled with it and got upset enough to want to throw it in the air. For sure that chicken could fly! Thankfully, today I could cut the chicken with no problem.

Momma and Poppee introduced me to their relatives, and they all welcomed me with open arms. I have this memory of when we took a trip to Ohio to visit Momma's family. We all had our iced tea and meal on the picnic table in the backyard one evening. We had a nice time just being with each other in fellowship. The sky got darker and darker. Suddenly I spied something yellow that kept flicking in the air. I was puzzled by what I had just seen and asked Momma what that was.She looked and said,

"Oh, that's fireflies!" I had never seen that before and wanted to put them in a jar to take home. It was indeed a beautiful sight! Here I was fourteen years old and just started to discover many new different things. The three of us traveled together to Niagara Falls and Disney World, hiked, rode our bike, visited families, played the game of Pass the Pigs, and ate ice cream at Crescent Ridge which still is one of my favorite places along with Hillard's Chocolate.

As life went on, there was another moment that defined my future. I was in my bedroom and looked out of my window to the back yard. Momma came into my room, walked up to me, and tapped on my shoulder to get my attention. I turned around and looked at her. Momma wanted to know if I was interested in going to Champion. I was confused at first until she explained that it was a youth group at the church. She encouraged me to attend because it would be a great way to meet new friends at my age. I was a bit lonely. I wanted something more. I agreed to check out the Champions and learned that I was the only Deaf student there at that time. Momma was happy to interpret a few times until I was comfortable to attend on my own. I again was in awe of seeing a bunch of teenagers who hung out together and played games then gathered to listen and study God's Word. I loved it! I learned so much more about God's love for me. Since then, I have always attended any Champion events and the gatherings.

During the summer of 1995, I decided to accept Jesus as my personal savior. I believed with all my heart that He was with me from the first moment I took a breath when I arrived on Earth till now. I am the living proof. I was baptized in the pool at the Family Ministry Center. Unfortunately, the Family Ministry Center had removed the pool, and it is no longer there. If only these grounds could talk. The Family Ministry Center was my favorite place. It gave me so many wonderful memories. Before summer began, we used to meet at the church on Thursday nights. During the summer, we gathered in a big tent they had set up for us for morning service and to praise the Lord. After the service, we had different fun activities to pick out- be at the playground, shoot some baskets, play volleyball, and toss horseshoes. On Friday nights, we had Friday Night Live, and no, it is not a reference to the TV show that is also called that. Friday Night Live involved fellowship, God's Word, and worship for Champion teens and their friends. It was a great way for us not to do foolish stuff that could tempt us. We even had Vacation Bible School at Family Ministry Center for the teenagers while elementary age kids met at the church.

Here is a snippet of history that affected me to do the same. In 1990, young students in Burleson, Texas got together for a church conference where they came up with this idea called *See You at the Pole*. Students meet at the school's flagpole before school starts in the morning to pray for their friends, schools, and leaders. Our prayers ask

God to bring moral and spiritual awakening to campuses and countries. I had heard about it and decided in 1997 to lead the *See You at the Pole* at my high school. I had spoken with my friends and wanted to know if they would like to join me. I recall the look on their faces, and they nodded their heads. I was not sure if they would have followed through. I just had to wait and find out. I even made sure that I would have an interpreter ready for that morning. It started out with just me then a few students joined me. There were no more than ten people gathered around the flagpole to pray for our school, teachers, our country, and so forth. It had taken a lot of prayer for God to give me the courage to ask my friends if they wanted to join me. Matthew 18:20 (NIV) in the bible states, "For where two or three gather in my name, there am I with them." I led the prayers with the students, and the principal came out to ask what we were doing. I told him, "We are praying for you and the school." He said, "Thank you" and left us alone. He just wanted to make sure that we would be in class on time. Whew, I thought we would be in trouble! I did not know what my friends had thought about the principal's visit, but I was so thankful for their bravery to join me.

I went to another youth conference called "Acquire the Fire." I was truly blessed by my youth pastor's support especially when he made sure I had an interpreter for different events. There was a time he got upset because the interpreter did not show up. He did the best he could. On the fun side, we often teased each other about whose high school was the best. Bristol-Plymouth Regional Technical School was where I attended while Southeastern Regional Vocational Technical High School was where my youth pastor and Poppee attended. These two schools were rivals. Luckily, I love those crazy people.

I guess when you grow up in the same environment, you start to talk, act, and do things like your family. However, when I lived with my foster family whose looks were hugely different from mine, people quizzed on who I was with. They asked whether she was my aunt or someone else. I told them that she is my Momma. Confusion quickly showed up on their face, and they tried not to look like a fool. So, they fumbled and said, "Oh, I see a resemblance." I usually rolled my eyes. Really, how so? Maybe our sense of humor and the fact that we use sign language for communication? I just wish people would not make that kind of statement. We are humans, and we sometimes say things that we wish we could have taken back.

While I lived with Momma and Poppee, I did try to stay in touch with my adopted family. The distance between us was challenging enough. I tried to call home or visit them. It took some time before I was able to finally meet up with my adoptive brothers. I remember the very first visit with my brothers after I moved in with my foster family. We had to meet at the Social Service building where social workers put us in a room with a glass window for them to observe us. It was very awkward. My brother, Joey, and I had a lot to talk about, but we did not feel we had the privacy to talk freely. The younger brothers, Henry and Andy, played with cars and trucks. They were too young to understand the whole situation. There was not enough time for Joey and me to catch up and for Joey to share the real updates about Mommy and daddy at home. That is a downside for us being in separate homes.

After the supervised visit, my brothers and I did not want to experience that again. We both did not feel comfortable in that room with a huge glass window. It was a bit creepy. It was only a matter of time when we would be able to meet again. Though I remember a time when Andy stayed with me for a sleepover at my foster home with Momma and Poppee. Many years later, I asked Andy if he remembered that visit. Andy told me that he cried a lot of times and wanted me to come back to his home. He mentioned about the stuffed animal I got him. It was a dog dressed up in hip hop style clothing. The dog also had shades. He carried it everywhere he went. One thing that stood out in Andy's mind was how many stuffed animals I had all over the house! That was true. I enjoyed collecting teddy bears, and they were all strewn over my bed.There was one in a pretty tea hat and fancy dress from Ms. Rosy and another in a cheerleader outfit that was a special gift from Poppee.

Then there wasa huge panda bear from my high school sweetheart. They are all gone now, but those were sweet memories.

After months of prayers for God's intervention, Mommy and daddy were no longer together. Mommy was doing well. She was studying to become a nurse; so, she and the boys moved back to the apartment with Grandma and Vavó . Joey worked for the Boys & Girls Club, and the younger kids did their own thing. Mommy allowed me to visit and take the boys out for some fun. We went to Big Top Playland, a Chuck E Cheese Knockoff in Fall River, Massachusetts. We played some games, had pizzas, and laughed a lot. They needed that to get the house of the darkness out of their system.

Mommy and I rebuilt our relationship, and I got to know her all over again. She still loved to laugh, jammed to music, and cooked her favorite meal - chicken pot pie. One of my favorite memories of my time with Mommy was when we went to Dunkin Donuts to hang out and have our iced coffee. Trust and respect gradually grew for each other. Once, when I visited her, she pulled me aside because she wanted to speak to me privately. She seemed so nervous, and I was anxious to understand what she wanted to share. Mommy told me she was proud of me and of how well I did in life. She wanted me to always remember to be strong.

As she talked, she pulled something out of her pocket and handed it to me. It was one of her engagement rings from her previous relationship, and she wanted me to have it. I thanked her and hugged her. I love Mommy for her boldness. I believe she did everything she could to take care of me. I added that ring to my necklace with my heart locket that had a picture in it of me with my birth mom. I have other charms that also represented who I was growing up. They felt like band aids over the old wounds, and the wounds healed over time.

Chapter 7

College Journey

So much had happened in the years since I lived with Momma and Poppee. They had two younger children; Jessica was only 2 years old when I left, and Craig was only one month old. Jessica liked to come into my room as soon as she woke up in the mornings. She loved to play with my stuffed animals, especially the big panda bear. There were never any dull moments with my little sister.

I graduated high school in 1998 and left home for Gallaudet University in Washington, D.C. Momma stayed home with the two little ones while Poppee drove me to Washington, D.C. On the road, we listened and sang to the good ole Oldies music, chatted a little, and acted silly a lot. There were lots of these moments with Poppee. When we arrived at the university campus, we went to the Hall Memorial Building to get information about the New Student Orientation week. We then drove to the parking lot under the Cogswell building to carry up my things to my dorm room. I did not yet know who my roommate would be but was excited at how big the room was.

We brought the last bag to my room then it was time for Poppee to say goodbye. He hugged me and left to start his long drive back to New England. After Poppee left, the room felt eerie, quiet, and lonely. My roommate did not arrive on campus until a few days later because she traveled from Canada. I felt isolated in the world of the unknown, not knowing what would happen in the next 5 minutes. Here I was in Washington, D.C., without a plan except for my studies. Now what? I decided to take it one day at a time.

My first week comprised of orientation sessions and placement tests for Math and English. Before I left New England, Momma told me not to get distracted with too many activities, but instead focus on my education. I was always busy with sports, church-related events, work, and high school. Being on Gallaudet campus, I knew no one and had little to do. A few days later, I saw a flier for the Bison Cheerleader tryout and thought, "What a great way to meet and make friends!" Despite Momma's suggestion, I tried out for Gallaudet cheerleader, made the team, and immediately found new friends. I must admit it was quite different from the high school cheerleading experience.

I was the only Deaf student on the team in high school. To make sure that I did the right movements, another cheerleader stood next to me to alert me which cheer was next. She prepped me, and we performed the steps together. Thank you, Cheerleader D., for all your help. I was a cheerleader for both the football and basketball teams. Being the only Deaf person on the team can be challenging. We did a lot of vocal chants. Once, during the basketball season, each cheerleader had to do a cheer with a different basketball player 's name in it. When it was my turn, I was not able to make out who was the player that I had to include in my cheer. I gave it all my best. Still the cheerleaders laughed at me. In general, I preferred not to use my voice during the cheer and instead did only body movement to avoid being a laughingstock again. I was a cheerleader during my sophomore and junior years.

During my senior year, I did not continue with cheerleading because I wanted to keep my promise with my good friends to play volleyball. Those three friends were already on the varsity teams for volleyball and basketball. We were all in the same grade. Two of the friends were twin sisters, and the other one was my bestie, Y.B., from preschool. We had the same class in Physical Education, and they thought I played volleyball well enough to join them on the team. I made a promise to try out for it and ended up being on the volleyball team. Just not on the varsity team with my friends because it was my first year. It felt strange to be the only senior on the junior varsity team! Well, promise is promise, and I kept it.

During my experience as a Gallaudet cheerleader, we all used sign language. Some of us used our voice, and it did not matter what we sounded like because all of us were Deaf. Our cheerleader coach used a huge drum to give us the rhythm to allow us to feel the vibration and keep up the pace together. We practiced together and then after the practice, we shared feedback. One of the cheerleaders had feedback, and it was about me! That girl screamed at me. Whoa, girl! She did not like that I was not talkative, and that I did not offer any opinions. I came off quiet as a church mouse. Time was what I needed to warm up to new people then I would be more comfortable to speak my mind. As time progressed, our team relationship grew stronger and stronger to the point where we felt comfortable to give each other cool nicknames. "Bunny" was the nickname for me because my energy was just the same as the Energizer Bunny who is the battery mascot known for its' unstoppable endurance.

Our team eventually became family. Together we celebrated our birthdays and went to clubs for good times especially for dancing! There was never a dull moment with the team. Remember I learned how to crochet? One of my cheerleader stuntmen learned how to crochet from me in our one-on-one sessions. I still have the photo of us. He did a great job! I wonder if he still has that blanket. Only he and the Lord know right now.

During the Christmas break, we all flew back home to be with our families for the holiday. I returned to Momma and Poppee's home, and it was wonderful to see everyone again. It was wonderful seeing my little sister, Jessica, who was thrilled to see me. She constantly said, “Mimi” as she followed me everywhere. We played together and opened the Christmas gifts. One of the gifts Jessica got was a Po from the Teletubbies. Do any of you remember that weird show? I much preferred Barney from the Barney & Friends. Barney was a cool purple dinosaur who sang the popular lyrics of I Love You. That show meant so much to me for different reasons. One of the reasons is it brings back special memories I had with my little brothers from my adoption family when we watched it together. So, with the foster family, it was the Teletubbies.

My baby brother, Craig, also had my attention. I held him a lot, and I remember his blue eyes with his captivating smile. I was able to give our parents some time alone to do their things, and I had the honor to babysit the kids on New Year 's Eve to let their parents go over to their neighbor 's home for some adult time. The holiday break was exactly what I needed to have a nice break with no agenda. The athletes including cheerleaders were expected to return to school campus earlier than others to practice and prepare for the upcoming game. Once again, my family and I said our goodbyes.

Cheerleaders reunited and went to Field House which was the gym at the time for us to do our practices. Afterwards, we planned to eat out for dinner at Uno's because the cafeteria was still closed for the winter break. After our dinner, some of us decided to visit a club. We returned to the dorm to change our outfits then met at one of the cheerleaders' friend's house. At the house, there were more people, and I just met some of them for the first time that night. We were ready to hit the club to have some fun, and this fella who I had just met at the house, came along with us. When we arrived at the club, the vibrations of the music moved our feet, and we danced through the night! We had to stop only because the club was ready to close for the night. None of us drove that night; so, we took the cab to return to our campus and that guy had decided to join us in the cab.

The campus was pretty much empty except for those athletes. I was one of the very few who was a freshman while others were upperclassmen. I strolled to my dorm only to find that the guy from the house was right behind me. He persistently followed me and he made some conversations, and I tried to be courteous. Still, he was like a sticky gum. I could not shake him off. I wanted to head up to my room. When I opened my door, he followed closely enough to help himself in. He forced his mouth onto mine and touched me where I did not want to be touched. I wanted to scream, but it was futile! There was no one on the floor, and the residential assistant was still away on the holiday break. I stumbled back and tried to fight him off. I clearly told him to stop. He did not care to pay attention to my pleas, and he was so intent to satisfy his own selfish needs. He refused to stop. I freaked out. Never had I thought that the word, rape, would become a reality for me. He raped me. He added more hatred to his crime; he smiled at me when he completed his goal. Then he left. I was so scared and pushed myself into denial. I thought, "Did this really just happen to me?"

I quickly grabbed my towel and shower caddy then rushed to the community bathroom in the residence hall to get in the shower and scrub the nasty stuff off me. I scrubbed endlessly, cried my eyes out, and felt so ashamed. I thought about Momma's suggestion. I thought if I had listened to her, I would not have been in this situation. In a way I felt like this was God's punishment for me that I had disobeyed Momma.

The very next day was the game day, and it was away. I had to drag myself out of my bed where I had crawled into after my hard, scrub down shower. I sobbed continuously and still felt ashamed of what just had happened a few hours ago. I reluctantly got dressed into my cheerleader uniform, and I no longer felt beautiful anymore. I grabbed my bag with me and headed out to meet the rest of the girls in front of Benson Hall circle, one of the popular meeting spots on campus. My movements became robotic. Our bus arrived, and we went in it. I stayed silent. I did not know what I should say or even do. My mind zoned out and felt so numb. I also felt unworthy of anything. I just wanted to shut the world out and be left alone. Usually I, the Bunny, was a highly spirited person and always positively boosted the team's spirit. None of that happened on that game day.

During the bus ride, even that same friend who in the beginning chewed me out for being too quiet came up to me and asked, "Kimmy, are you OK?" I cried and told her what had happened. She said she was sorry and empathically understood my situation. She, herself, was raped, too. Of course, she had to inform our cheerleader head coach. My coach and I spoke privately. She recommended that I sit this game out, and I took her advice. I sat on the bleacher away from the team who got on the floor to do their cheering routines. I thought I looked horrible and that I could not muster up any effort to do my best. How could I? Obviously, the other cheerleaders wanted to know why I sat this one out. Thankfully, my head coach gave me the support that I needed. She told them not to worry about it and to give me the space.

We had a tradition that whenever we go to an away game, we stopped by a 7-11 to get soda and snacks after the game. It did not matter if we won or lost the game. Nevertheless, a trip to 7-11 was our reward. We even came up with our own cheer chant for 7-11! Back then, a treat from 7-11 was a luxury trip! Anything but cafeteria food! That night, I decided to seek comfort in a whole lot of chocolates and Coca-Cola soda.

The second semester had officially started on the schedule. Students and staff returned to the campus. I was thrilled to see my friends again and my roommate, Shorty. Shorty and I talked about the latest news about ourselves. Yet, I opted not to tell her about my nightmare. During our conversation, the light in our room flashed on and off. Someone rang our doorbell. I went to look though the peep hole and to my terror, he was right there at my door! The rapist who viciously took my innocence! I was mortified and hid in my closet. Shorty answered the door to let him know that I was not here. I was so shaken up and scared. I really did not want to face him. Shorty opened my closet door and demanded that I explain what in the world just happened. She had never seen me so scared before.

Let me tell you something about my roommate. She may be short, but the Puerto Rican in her blood made her a mama bear. No one wants to mess with her. I finally shared with her about my situation with that guy. That mama bear in her came out roaring. She told me that I must report to the Department of Public Safety (DPS). Thankfully, she was with me when I reported to the DPS. The officer asked questions, and I answered them all. Then I gave the rapist's name to the officer. He pulled up his file and to my surprise, his file was so thick. Apparently, it was not his first time he had raped someone here on this campus. So that means I was not his first victim. Sadly, he used to work for the president of Gallaudet University. I asked the officer what I should do next. He said because I washed away the evidence, and it had been a few days since that night of the rape all I could do was to take him to court, and I decided to do that. Though when that court date arrived, my fears and doubts crept up into my mind as I walked up the steps to the court building. I froze. I felt so small as I stood before the huge building. I could not bring myself into the building and into the courtroom. I still felt overwhelmingly ashamed and did not want others to know about me. I chickened out, walked back down the steps, and left. I did not want to face this alone. Still to this day as I wrote this in the year of 2021, I do not know what happened to the rapist in that courtroom on that day 23 years ago.

My focus on school dwindled and soon, I lost my motivation for anything. I tried to heal myself from what that guy did to me. Not only that, I also struggled with my identity. Who was I? Where did I belong? I felt lost. At that time, my relationship with Mommy was still in the rebuilding stage and I tried to stay in touch with my brothers, too. Not only that, I also tried to figure out what was my role with my foster family. Do not get me wrong. I am forever grateful that Momma and Poppee opened their home for me. Just some situations did not sit well with me, mostly between me and Momma. Poppee was mostly quiet and talked when it was necessary. It might be because Momma could speak my language in American Sign Language. My 'honeymoon' phase with them changed the last three years of my high school when I lived with them. I felt torn on where I fit in with different backgrounds and different family situations. I worried constantly about my adoptive family. Then one evening at dinner time, I made a comment that someone at my school asked me if my foster parents will have a child of their own. Imagine my shock and confusion when Momma responded, "Yes, we are! I am pregnant." I looked at Poppee. His eyes looked like they were ready to pop out! I guess he did not expect this kind of announcement at dinner!

Momma was taken aback of my reaction and said, "What?" I didn't even congratulate them. I made sure they knew I was furious. I could not finish my dinner and ran off to work. At that time, I worked for Shaw's Supermarket. I first began as a bagger then got a transfer to a bakery department. I loved my bakery job. Now whenever I walk by the bakery department, I smile and remember the fond memories.

Back to that night, I calmed down when I got home from work. I learned that Momma was not supposed to tell me about her pregnancy until much later. We had some discussion, and in that discussion, she shared with me of how far along she was in her pregnancy. I was surprised. It used to be just three of us - Momma, Poppee, and I. Now with the baby on the way, I shared my fear about being nobody or that the sense of belonging I had would be taken away. It took a while for me to get used to this new change. Momma had several baby showers, and Poppee encouraged me to attend one of those. I did not go to any of the showers except for the last one. Believe it or not, the shower was at the same school where I used to attend pre- kindergarten. Momma probably thought by now that I was not going to be at any of the showers. I am known to stage surprises. I hid behind the door, and as soon as she walked in, I jumped out to greet her. She was surprised and immediately hugged me. At the time, I still struggled about my role with the foster family and struggled about being away from my adoptive family. I felt torn and guilty of my blessings with my foster family whereas my adoptive family struggled with life.

Months later, the baby was ready to come out and meet us! We went to the hospital and settled into the room to be ready for the birth. Talk about the awkward moments! The nurse asked me if I had planned to stay in the room and observe the birthing process. We did not even cross that bridge to talk about that part! I tried to stay angry with Momma but decided to throw that attitude out of the window. It was time for me to put my feelings aside. Momma was fine if I decided to stay in the room for the birth, and Poppee felt the same. Boy, I had no idea what I had gotten myself in to be part of it. Momma gave all her best to bring the baby into the world, but it was not meant to be. Off she went into another room to be prepped for a C-Section.

I was Poppee's cheerleader to ease his nervousness and spent my time in the waiting room. I was anxious for the announcement. Finally, Poppee came out of the operating room, and he was still dressed up in scrubs. I looked at him as if I wanted to know if it was a boy or girl. Poppee told me it was a girl!! I left Poppee and tried to find Momma and my baby sister. When I finally found their room, I walked in and saw a tiny baby girl right next to Momma. I was amazed by how tiny she was! I strongly believe that being part of the birthing process healed the rift I felt in my heart about the latest changes with my foster family.

Few months later, the director of Regional Educational Assessment & Diagnostic Services (R.E.A.D.S.) asked me if I was interested being in competition for the Miss Deaf Massachusetts Pageant. I honestly did not think I was qualified to be allowed into the competition because I was simply an ordinary young woman. I told the director that I would be honored to be part of the pageant. With the short notice, I had so much to do to get ready for it! Momma and I searched at a thrift shop to find a dress for formal wear. I absolutely love shopping at the thrift store! You cannot beat their fantastic prices! Does anyone agree with me? Our search was a success! We found a simple green sleeveless dress with the top part of the dress embodied with beads. It was so pretty, and the best part of it, I felt so comfortable in it! It just needed some hemming work. We had planned to have that done on one Sunday after the church service. The plan was for Momma and Poppee to drive separate cars to get to church then split up after the service. I rode with Momma to church, and we got into an argument! She said some things that were hurtful. She is a Christian, but that did not mean she was a perfect holy human. None of us are. Only God is perfect.

When Momma pulled up into the parking lot at church, she told Poppee to take me home. I was shocked and mad as well! Poor Poppee did not know what had just happened and did what she asked to take me home. As soon I got into the house, I called Mommy to get me. I was so upset and fed up with being in the middle of the two families. I had no tolerance for anyone to talk negative or trashy about my adoptive family. No ONE is above anyone. Each of us possesses unique skills, and we are in this together as a whole family. Experience for each of us is different, and that does not give anyone the right to talk trash.

I called a cab service to send a cab to take me to aa meeting spot for Mommy to pick me up. She arrived with her new boyfriend, and I got into their car to head down to Fall River. Mommy asked what had happened with me earlier that morning. There was no way I wanted to share with her about the incident. I felt it was for the best to keep my mouth shut. If I had spilled the details, she would become furious with Momma. I did not want my two Mommies to get into an argument. Instead, I laid it all out with God. It was not easy for me to do so. I prayed for wisdom in my words and actions. I spent the day with my adoptive family.

The day was so lovely! It was terrific to be with Vavó again since we had not seen each other in a long while. She made my favorite foods, and together we watched the *Three Stooges*. I spent time together with my brothers, and I spent some quality time with Joey. Just when things rolled well, it was about to change in the next minute. As the sky got darker, someone showed up at the front door with a message from Momma. She sent my interpreter, Maddy, to deliver the Message, and the Message was straightforward "You either come home or do not come at all." Really? You had to threaten me. I felt awful that my interpreter was caught amid this. She had her own life, and Momma could have shown up to say that herself. Nothing made sense. I had to think and pray for a minute since I did not like this threat. I concluded that the right thing to do was to go back home. Wherever that home was lately! I said goodbyes to my adoptive family and told them to keep in touch.

Let's say it was not an easy car ride home. We talked very little. When I arrived home, Maddy wished me the best of luck and left. I slowly dragged myself into the house. Poppee and Momma waited in the kitchen for my arrival. Momma said we had to talk now. Our talk began with a warning that I was not allowed to ever do that again or otherwise, I am to leave their house for good. It was so hard to hear this from her. My feelings got all jumbled up. My thought was that they welcomed me into their house with acknowledgment that I came with a lot of baggage. I have family from my past and other family in front of me. I did not want to cut the rope from them. It is not acceptable for me if anyone talks awful about anyone in both adoptive and foster families. It is not how we show love toward one another. Momma's comments threw me off more especially because this happened in a Christian home.

Through all this mess, I had a high school boyfriend that I could seek solace in his arms. I needed that mental break and some room to breathe. Being with my boyfriend's family showed me what a real family looks like. Though do not get me wrong, I love all my families. They are part of who I am today. I just cannot stand having to choose between Mommy and Momma. It got so confusing to battle my feelings of where I stand in a huge family. It made my head spin uncontrollably. At the time, I was so ready to go to college to take the time to figure out myself. I put myself last when I tried to please everyone. It was about time to think for myself. I had to figure out what was the best for my mental and my soul.

In the meantime, my struggles I had at college affected my ability to make decisions about the future. On one hand, I am forever grateful that the foster family had opened their home to me and showed me their love. On the other hand, I still felt something was missing. I had to decide which subject to major in at Gallaudet. What did I want to be? Studio Artist? Teacher for the Deaf? Business Marketer? I was more afraid to choose one because then I would be stuck with it for the rest of my life. I was not ready for that kind of commitment. I realized then that I wanted to explore and experience more things in life. I needed the Lord's guidance and wisdom in my next steps. I had to count on the Lord every day, every hour, every minute, and yes, every second.

Chapter 8

If Only He Knew

Anger and confusion grew more and more as I struggled as a college student. Still had no idea what to major in for my degree. Honestly, I felt like I wasted time and money to take any course that may not be counted toward a specific degree. I could not deal with another minute of confusion. Momma and Poppee noticed the decline in my effort in all classes and wanted me to return home for the weekend. I agreed. My mind needed a break. I had hoped that the short break would help me see the light and get a clear picture of my future goals. I packed my bag and hopped on the train to head back to New England. Momma met me at the train station and took me home. Even though I may have changed, I knew Momma and Poppee still welcomed me home with open arms again.

I went into my bedroom and stood in the middle of the room. As I strolled through reflections of my life, my emotions overtook me, and I felt unworthy. I became doubtful of myself and wondered what my purpose in this life was. Eventually I broke down and cried. Momma must have heard me because she came into my room. As soon as she hugged me, I let it all out including about that night how the rapist destroyed my spirit. As soon as Poppee heard about that night, he grew furious at the situation. I admit it was a positive change for a father figure like Poppee who stood up for me, believed in me, and showed me genuine support. In the past, other father figures abused me. Poppee never did that. Yes, he was known to be quiet, but his actions spoke louder. I am forever thankful that the Lord had placed him in my life. Momma suggested that we should pray for God's guidance and to ask God to grant me the sense of peace. After we prayed, we all hugged in silence, and Poppee left my room to give the ladies some time alone.

When Sunday came along, we went to church. It was good to see some of my high school friends and my youth pastor again. I noticed during the visit at Brockton Assembly of God that the church had made some changes. I remember a secretary there who always greeted anyone who came into church. It did not matter to her what background we came from, and she always loved you for who you are. It was indeed great seeing her again. After the service, I was scheduled to meet with my youth pastor to talk about my complicated situation. On my way to the pastor's office, I ran into my high school sweetheart. We had already broken up about a year before I went to college. We made small chit chat. He questioned how I had been doing and how college life had been for me. I kept our conversation short and simple and shared only the good highlights of my life. He shared about his work and how he enjoyed being with his friends.

While he talked, I couldn't help but wonder if only he knew the real reason why I was in town. Would he still love me - this girl with a messy life? Even when we dated in high school, I never told him the reason why I went to live with my foster family. He knew nothing about my upbringing and certainly not the college life I had. His life seemed so easy, carefree, peaceful, and fun compared to mine. We wrapped up our chat and said our goodbyes. That moment reminded me of Reba McEntire's song called *And Still.* The song is about a guy who asked a girl how she had been, and she lied. I was that girl. I made the decision to leave him in the past because I felt in my heart that I was not good enough for him. And I believed with all my heart that the Lord had someone better for him, and indeed He did.

Afterwards, I went to my youth pastor's office with Momma. He asked to share what had been on my mind. I held back nothing and told him what the rapist had done to me. The last thing I expected to come out of my pastor's mouth was this next question! He said, "Have you forgiven him?" Yo! What did you just ask me?! I thought out aloud, "Not after what he did to me, why in the world will I ever forgive him. NO WAY! I love you. But have you lost your mind, Pastor?" He looked at me with compassion and understanding about my feelings. He did not blame me for my reaction. He then showed me a couple verses in the Bible on how we should handle this kind of situation. Believe me, it was not an easy thing to read.

"For if you forgive other people when they sin against you, your heavenly Father will also forgive you." Matthew 6:14 (NIV)

"Do not judge, and you will not be judged. Do not condemn, and you will not be condemned. Forgive, and you will be forgiven." Luke 6:37 (NIV)

The Pastor, Momma, and I prayed together for God's guidance, to heal my heart and mind, and for me to find willingness to forgive my enemy. I cried again when the Pastor comforted me with a hug. For a long time, I felt there was a black heavy cloud above me. Even though people were happy to see me again, I gave them a false impression that all was well with me. It was good to see family and friends again, but I had to go back to Gallaudet that night.

I tried to get myself together again and try life again. I was still a cheerleader for the basketball team. After a game, some of the cheerleaders wanted to head out to the nightclub and asked if I wanted to go with them. It took me a moment to think whether I really wanted to go or not. I then decided to join my gals. I went to my dorm to get out of my uniform and into nightclub clothing to join my girls. When we arrived at the nightclub, there were a lot of people on the dance floor. I joined them to jam and sing aloud to some of the lyrics to the song. Thankfully, people cannot hear how badly I sang over the loud music. As I moved around the dance floor, I froze when I saw someone. There he was - the rapist who took my soul and my EVERY THING!

I felt the temperature in me rising and wanted to punch him so badly. I knew that was not going to make things better. I decided to try to remain calm and be alert. When he saw me, he did something that I never thought he would have the guts to do. He came and said, "I am sorry for what I did to you. I hope you can forgive me." What the heck?! I tried so hard to control my emotions. My mind was suddenly filled with so many thoughts of what to say or do. Slowly, my anger cooled off when I realized I was not alone. Do you want to know what I said?

I forgave him. Yes, I did. True, I could beat him up right there and not forgive him. Instead, the Holy Spirit was with me. I felt calm. After I gave him my forgiveness, we went on our own way. Imagine if I had not gone to that club that very night, I would have missed the opportunity to see him and release him from my anger.

Also, I felt if I had not forgiven him, he might do it again, and I would carry around this heavy weight on my shoulder. Since the Lord gave me the strength to forgive him, I never saw him again. I felt God did not want me to carry my burden anymore. I felt led to let it go and let GOD handle the rest. I kid you not, it was not an easy thing to do that yet that was the BEST thing I ever did for myself. I found peace! 1 Peter 5:7-11 encourages me, and I want to share it with you. "Give all your worries and cares to God, for he cares about you. Stay alert! Watch out for your great enemy, the devil. He prowls around like a roaring lion, looking for someone to devour. Stand firm against him and be strong in your faith. Remember that your family of believers all over the world is going through the same kind of suffering you are. In his kindness God called you to share in his eternal glory by means of Christ Jesus. So, after you have suffered a little while, he will restore, support, and strengthen you, and he will place you on a firm foundation. All power to him forever! Amen." 1 Peter 5:7-11 (NLT)

God wanted me to cast all my anxiety and burden onto HIM - God. Why? Because He cares for you and me! He loves us so much. It is as if he said this to me, "Kimmy, my dear Daughter, please TRUST me and let ME handle this MY way, for I know what exactly to do. Stop trying to handle it your way because it does not work out that way." God said so in Jeremiah 29:11 (NIV) "For I know the plans I have for you," declares the Lord, "plans to prosper you and not to harm you, plans to give you hope and a future.

Chapter 9

Summertime

I made the decision to stay in Washington, D.C. after my meeting with my youth pastor. I needed the time to figure myself out. Who was I exactly? What was my identity? Adopted family. Foster family. Biological family. I concluded that I needed to stay where I was and figure it out on my own, with the Lord's help. For the remainder of my freshman year, I decided to try out for a part in *Rathskeller*. J. K. describes it the best in his words of what *Rathskeller* is all about, "It was an American Sign Language (ASL) performance art that was created in 1998 to showcase the raw beauty of sign language by combining it with visual arts and pulsating music. It turned out to astonish crowds and quickly became internationally known for thrilling levels of originality and intensity, which are rarely seen in ASL productions."

I had an audition at the end of the year and made it! As a matter of fact, I was the youngest and probably the naivest in the group. I had an amazing experience. I got to travel to Sweden, Denmark, Canada, and across America. The best part was I got to be with my real good friend, Raina. We made a deal. She already had a part in *Gallaudet Dance Company*, and I already had my part with *Rathskeller*. The deal was for me to try out for the part in *Gallaudet Dance Company, and for her* to try out for the part in *Rathskeller*. We amazingly made it in and performed for both companies together!

On July 1, 2000, Rathskeller was scheduled to perform for the Summer Festival in Milwaukee, Wisconsin. We arrived a day earlier. Raina and I were filled with excitement and got the backstage passes to Morris Day and the Time!!! They performed at 10 pm and invited us to dance on the stage with them. It was as if we had our own jam session! Then when they were done, their invitation extended to hang out with them afterwards. It turned out we stayed at the same hotel! We chilled out in a bar at the hotel and chatted away until the sunrise.

The next day, more like the next few hours since we stayed up all night, Raina and I were still high with excitement. We were roommates at the hotel, and we barely slept at all. We talked about our time with Morris Day and his guitarist. I have to say this again, we stayed up the whole night! Did this just happen to us? Out of all ladies, Morris Day and his guitarist chose to stay and talk with us. We had to pinch ourselves to make sure it was not a dream. With all that excitement, we went down to eat breakfast and get ready for our performance in the evening.

We, the Rathskeller cast, headed out to the festival. There was a stage for many different Deaf performances. There was a Deaf drummer in his solo act then there was a group of Deaf men dancers called the *Wild Zappers*. They did many different dance performances. I already knew two of the guys in that group. I met them the year before in the summer through the Young Scholar Program in Model Secondary School for The Deaf. It was the summer when I learned so much about Mexico's culture and their dances. It was an experience, I truly enjoyed myself with new friends.

Like I said, I had never heard of Wild Zappers and was amazed by their performances. Raina knew all the dancers of the Wild Zappers and introduced me to one of the dancers who she called daddy. She called him daddy because he played a huge role in her life as a father figure. His real name was Wawa. He was a true gentleman and had a beautiful smile. Boy, he sure was handsome! I kept my cool. I told him my name and that it was my pleasure to meet him. Raina had not seen Wawa for a long time due to his busy traveling schedule and performances; she wanted to spend more time with daddy to catch up on news in their lives. I tagged along with Raina, and through their conversation, I had learned that Wawa had just flown in from Japan only two days ago, and he was an uncle of twin nephews. He was so proud to be their uncle and loved to spoil them.

It was time for us to get back to our trailer to get ready for our performance. Wawa was already in the trailer reading his book. Raina needed to iron her clothes, and I did too. As I was waiting for my turn, I decided to use the time to talk with Wawa to get to know him more. I noticed Raina gave me the side looks, and I did not know why. When we were on our way to our stage, Raina told me that she could not believe how open I was with him. She knew I typically kept things to myself, and I did not allow any guys to get close to me. After the traumatic experience with the rapist, I had a fear that the incident might happen to me again. I made the decision to shut down and tell the guys to get out of my business, except I did not feel any threat when I was with Wawa. There was something unique about this dude. During our performance, I saw Wawa in the back of the audience, and he smiled. In that very moment when I was dancing, I kicked my leg up, and my black boot flew off my foot! I died on the inside with embarrassment but did not stop my performance. Somehow, I got my black boot back. Thank you to whoever brought it back to me.

After the performance, Wawa came up to the cast and told us that we did a great job. He added that he did enjoy that part of the flying boot! Oh, Lawd, have mercy. The Wild Zappers and Rathskeller crews got together to stroll around the festival. The atmosphere was filled with jamming music, and there were carnivals, food trucks, and clothing and craft booths. After the closing hour, we rode back to our hotel and decided to hang out together.

We ordered pizza and continued conversations. Time got away from us, and it was time for us all to head back to our rooms. I chatted with Raina and reflectedon our weekend. It was the bomb! We both had a wonderful time.

The next day, we packed up and had breakfast at the hotel before we left for our flights. I sat down next to Wawa. He was on my right while Raina was on my left. During my talk with Rainia, and of all these days, it had to be that day I accidentally knocked down my drink. Guess whose side my drink spilled over to? Wawa's side! I was mortified. Wawa was a gentleman, kept his cool, and helped me clean up my mess. I felt horrible and offered endless apologies! He laughed and told me it was not a problem. First my boot, then the drink! Surely, I gave him a great first impression.

Before we left for the airport, Wawa and I took several pictures together. Remember this was back in 2000; more than 20 years ago when there was no cell phone with photo capability like today. We used an old disposable camera. Oh, the good ole days. Unfortunately, I do not have these photos. I lost the film roll. Prior to our departure, Wawa and I discovered that we lived not too far away from each other. We agreed we could stay connected when we got back home and walked away. The Wild Zappers and the Rathskeller used differentairlines. Raina and I thought we had a blast and an unforgettable weekend.

When I arrived in D.C., I shared my experience with my roommates Shorty and K.C. Shorty had to calm me down because I was on 'cloud nine' from the trip. I could not get it out of my mind, and I wanted to reach out to him. Since we did not have a computer in our apartment, my roommate and I had to walk to Gallaudet campus to use the computer in the Hall Memorial Building. This was way before Facebook chats and text messages; we used AOL Instant Messages (AIM). I left a message for Wawa, and he responded back quickly! I screamed and was surprised that he responded to me! My roommate, Shorty, was there with me and told me to be quiet. I was not able to contain my excitement. I went to a window and screamed!! Praise the Lord since it was a DEAF university. No one could hear me. Whew! On July 4th, we had arranged to meet and watch the fireworks together with Raina and our other friends. For some reason, Wawa and I had missed each other, and I was a little bummed out. Regardless, Raina and I still had a fun time with our friends, and I went back to my apartment.

The next day, Wawa and I called each other to make another attempt to meet again. This time without crowds! He lived in Greenbelt, Maryland and I lived near Gallaudet. We both decided that it was best to meet at a bookstore in Union Station. After I hung up the phone, Iscreamed with excitement, again Shorty told me to be quiet. Notice how I screamed a lot? Could you blame me?

I did not know at that time that Wawa was 'famous' in the Deaf Community, and this famous guy made the time to be with me! K.C. rooted for me. I quickly got ready. I put on my casual fancy clothes and painted my face with makeup. There was no way I would meet Wawa in time if I used D.C.'s public transportation. K.C. graciously offered to give me a lift to Union Station. As we arrived in front of the Union Station building, she wished me luck and took off.

By now my palms felt sweaty, and I had butterflies in my stomach. I gave myself a pep talk. Am I really going to meet him? I had to pinch myself. GULP! Well, there was no turning back now. I hurried to the bookstore and found that Wawa had not arrived yet from the metro train. While I waited for his arrival, I decided to just roam around in the bookstore. He arrived, and we hugged each other. We decided to take a walk around outside in front of Union Station. It was a nice and cool night with stars in the sky. We walked and talked to get to know each other more. The sky got darker, and it was a bit hard to see Wawa as he talked. It was as if he blended into the sky, and only saw his eyes that looked like the eyes of Cheshire cat from a Disney story called Alice in Wonderland.

When he noticed my struggle to make out what he said, he politely walked under the light post. Voila! Now I can see him. I was a little embarrassed and did not have the courage to ask him to come into the light like Belle asked the Beast in the Disney movie, *Beauty and the Beast.* No, Wawa was nothing like a Beast. I just did not want to sound rude. We laughed a lot. We talked so much that we became hungry. We both walked back to Union Station to eat at a restaurant there. The night got away from us. It was time to go home. Wawa walked me out to hail for a cab. We bid our farewell, and he took the metro back home. He was absolutely a gentleman. He opened the door, allowed me to walk in front of him, and pulled out the chair for me. I was flattered.

My roommates waited up for me. Shorty was the protective one. She was with me when I dealt with the rape situation and wanted to make sure I do not experience anything like that again. I understood why she acted like that. After all, no one messes with the girl from the Bronx. K.C. was from the countryside and was a true hopeless romantic. They listened as I shared details of my romantic evening then we drifted off to sleep.

Wawa and I got in touch again soon after that date to plan for another date. We decided to attend a nightclub. This night club had three floors that played several types of music such as R&B, Hispanic and Hip Hop. My roommates and friends from Gallaudet went there, too. I remember there was one dance area that had mirrors on the walls. Wawa, this crazy dude, jammed to the music wildly and to embarrass me even more, he decided to dance with the huge speakers. I thought this man was crazy. Yes, we are Deaf, but even I could not get that close to the speakers. That was too loud! When I danced with Wawa, there was another guy who took my hand to dance with him. The guy tried to show Wawa how to dance properly, and Wawa took it well. He stood there to watch and nodded his head in a way that said, "Yeah. Ok, I got this." Then the guy gave me back to Wawa. My friends laughed at his silliness. I know and believe he could dance. Did I not just see his performance a few days ago? He could dance, but I did not understand why he acted like that.

After the dance, we went straight to the bar. He asked me if I wanted an alcoholic drink, and I replied, "No, because I could not." Then Wawa answered back, "Ok. If you are not going to drink, then I will not either." I told him that he could go ahead and order whatever he wanted to drink for himself. He would not have any of that. Instead, he ordered two sodas. When we got our sodas, I could not help but give away my puzzling look. I was a bit surprised that Wawa thought there was nothing wrong that I had said no to the alcoholic drink. I mustered up the courage to ask Wawa, "Do you know why I cannot have a drink?" He responded calmly and said, "Maybe it is because of your medical reason. I do not care. It is fine if you are not going to drink. I would not either." I finally told him the reason why I could not drink.

His body froze when he realized I was underage. He mentally prepared himself to make the choice of J.O.B. which stands for Jail or Bail! He asked slowly, “HOW…OLD…ARE…YOU?” After I told him that I was 20 years old, I asked for his age. Wawa answered like a daddy figure, “Hunny, I will be 30 in December!” Then it was my turn to freeze! My eyes popped out and tried to hold onto my can of Coca-Cola. I blurted out, “My Mommy is dating a guy who is the same age as you!” We looked at each other and thought we should see where this relationship goes for us.

We met in July, and our relationship became official a month later just before I left for a trip to Puerto Rico with my good friend who was like a brother to me. He had a kind heart and asked if I was interested in joining him on the trip. I said yes because I wanted to know more about my culture since my biological dad was from Puerto Rico. I found Puerto Rico to be incredibly beautiful upon my arrival. My “brother’s” cousin picked us up from the airport and drove to their grandfather’s house. His grandparents did not speak any English. I felt a bit uncomfortable because his grandfather just sat and stared at me. I spent most of the time in the bedroom when I was not outdoors. His grandparents lived in the middle of nowhere. Beautiful scenic view but not like downtown where there were plenty of things to do.

Few days later, his cousin took us horseback riding on a nice trail. I enjoyed it. After we were done with the horses, we went to the private beach. There was eerily no one there; just a few people who lived near the beach. We stayed there for a couple of hours then I was already ready to leave. Brother's cousin returned to pick us up and drove us back to his grandfather's house. We had dinner. I explained to my Brother, "Ok, I came here for vacation, not 'deathcation'. We have to do something before we fly out."

In our best attempt with the language barrier, we informed the grandparents that we were going out. Brother and I had absolutely no idea where we were going! We walked until we arrived at a village. We discovered a bar-like place that played music and had a nice pool table. We looked at each other and agreed to check this place out. We boldly walked in and ordered our drinks. After we got our drinks, we walked over to the pool table and played a few games. We also jammed to the music. At last, we had something to do other than being at the grandparents' house.

Few days later, we moved to his aunt's house. Her home had the luxurious touch of marble tiles on the floor and had a huge living room with tall windows. Aunt had two children, a boy and a girl. It was a very nice and relaxing place. We went to the beach and toured around San Juan. The city had small town shops, tasty food, and music. Soon we had to leave to fly home. Alas, we did not realize that our flight was during the hurricane season. Our flight was delayed, and we were stuck at the airport. Thankfully, we arrived back to Washington, D.C. just in time for us to start our fall semester at Gallaudet. Gallaudet had a commuter lodge where those who lived off campus could use the place to rest, study, and eat. Often my handsome boyfriend, Wawa, visited me in the commuter lodge. It was always a blessing to see Wawa there even though he was a busy guy.

Chapter 10

Our Gatherings

Wawa and I dated for about three months, and so far, it went well. We continued to learn more about each other, our weaknesses, and our strengths. Holidays were right around the corner. We made plans to drive up to Philadelphia for Thanksgiving then to New England for Christmas. I wanted to see where Wawa used to live and understand his background more. Wawa rented a car for us to use to get to Philadelphia. We hit the road and jammed to music together. Music was loud. LOUD! Wawa did his crazy dance moves again, and I really thought that he wanted to test me to see how well I could put up with this crazy nut.

As we got closer and closer to Wawa's home state within 15 minutes, I begged him to turn around and drive back to D.C.! He was like what?!! Have you lost your mind?! Yes!! I freaked out! God knows what else I felt that day. Again, I begged him to turn around and head back home. He had enough of my pleas and pulled over to a parking lot to calm me down. Yes, I certainly had a nervous breakdown! Wawa finally calmed me down and firmly encouraged me to meet his family. I did not want to see or hear anything more from his mouth and hands. Do not forget that we use hands for sign language. I told him to hush up and drive before I changed my mind. I felt so anxious to meet the rest of his family members. I had already met his Mom at an event. She was the reason why I was in Philadelphia!

About a month ago, his mom came down to Maryland to visit Wawa. I first met her at a mall where I felt safe and had the ability to turn around and RUN if our meeting was a disaster. It is safe to say I did not run. Later that evening, there was a banquet where Wawa was scheduled to do his performance, and we joined him there. I sat at a circular banquet table with his Mom next to me. Mind you, this was a Deaf event where the primary language was sign language. There were other Deaf folks at the table. At the table, I carried a conversation with a guy who did not use his voice and used sign language. Our conversation got to the point where he told me about his family upbringing and how many children there were in his family. Then out of nowhere, Wawa's mom said, "Wow, that's a lot of kids!" Imagine the shock on my face! Did she understand the whole conversation? I thought to myself that it was a good thing I did not say anything bad about her son! She might as well have slapped me silly. I had to excuse myself from the table to find Wawa! I walked up to him and said, "Wawa, why didn't you tell me that your mom can sign!?!" He only had one reply,

"Oh, I am sorry. I must have forgotten!" Really?! Argh! Luckily, he was so handsome that I could not stay mad at him for very long.

I walked back to the banquet table and resumed the evening. Wawa's mom had a great time. It was like two prices for one since it was her birthday as well. She enjoyed dressing up like a queen, enjoyed the meal, and the music as well. We got to see Wawa and his crew's smashing performance. When the banquet ended, we drove her back to her hotel. She was to leave the next day. As we bid our farewell, his mom asked him if he had planned to come home for Thanksgiving. Wawa answered with a yes. Then his mom told him, "Do not come home without her." He said OK. His mother said it again, and his response was the same. She said it again for the third time then he said, "OK. Mom, she is coming with me." She answered back, "That is what I wanted to hear." His mother needed solid confirmation by her son that he will bring a crazy woman from New England to Philadelphia for Thanksgiving. God, bless this woman.

So, here we were at his mother's house. His mom was elated to see me and hugged me for a long time. She gave me a tour of her home, and we talked like there was no tomorrow. The next day, Wawa had run to the store to buy a few belated birthday gifts for his twin nephews before they arrived for Thanksgiving dinner. While he was out on his errand run, I showered and got dressed for Thanksgiving dinner. I came down to help his mom in the kitchen. She said I did not have to dress up. Just be yourself. I looked at myself and told her that was how I dress. My clothes were not super fancy; just comfortable and casual. I sat on the kitchen stool as she prepared the food, and we took this opportunity to get to know each other better. She did not like the fact that I was a Patriot fan since she was an Eagle fan. Yeah, our teams really got along well…NOT! That sure kept the banter going in our conversation in the days to come.

When Wawa returned from his birthday shopping spree and walked in the kitchen, his mom and I stopped our conversation. Poor Wawa. He stood and looked at us. We looked back at him. He finally said, "Ok, I guess I will be out of your way." As soon as he stepped out of the kitchen, we went back to our conversation. More visitors arrived, and I got to meet his two sisters, the twin nephews, and his niece. Our time went so well. We jammed to music, and I danced with Wawa's niece who was about a year old. Oh, the soul food was so delicious. It was wonderful to meet the rest of Wawa's family and was able to see why they were a tight-knit family. They got through 'the good, the bad and the ugly' together, and they will always be family forever, no matter what.

They introduced 'Black Friday' to me. I had never heard of it as a popular shopping day. I guess it was a huge thing in Philadelphia. You can find things for dirt cheap, and it was a madhouse swarmed with people. They also introduced my stomach to the Philly cheesesteak. We visited downtown. I was in for some culture shock yet enjoyed myself. Through this trip, I understood Wawa better, and I saw that he was the same here as he was in Maryland. I thought he would behave differently elsewhere, but he did not. I was glad to see that. He was real from the start. He came off as an open book and left it up to me to either pick it up or close it. I decided to keep it open and read on the pages even when it was hard to read him at times.

November left and December came. It was my turn to bring Wawa up to New England to meet my adoptive family. I did not think at that time to have him meet my foster family just yet. We rented a car again. We did this a lot. We did not need to own a car because our lives in DC and Maryland relied on public transportations, train and bus, to get around the city.

As usual, we had the car radio on during our drive on I-95 North toward Massachusetts. As we approached New York, I did not know there were two different routes with I-95, top or the bottom. I admit I was horrible with directions! Thank goodness for today's GPS navigation! As I tried to figure out my way around, I hit a curb! Yup! We got a flat tire. I panicked and looked at Wawa for his reaction. I thought he would chew me out for not paying attention on the road. He simply calmed me and said, "It was alright." I wondered what really went on in his mind. Did he think to himself, "Gosh, this girl can't drive?" Wawa got out of the car to change the tire, and he sang as he changed the tire. Yes, you just read this correctly-he SANG! I would have handled it differently if I was in his shoes; I would definitely not sing happy tunes. Not Wawa. As soon as he finished the tire replacement, he kindly suggested that we should switch our seats. I was a wreck to continue with the drive. I gladly handed over the car key.

Wawa got us to our destination safely. Remember I had mentioned in the previous chapter that all my adoptive family lived in the same house but within their own apartment. Mommy's apartment was on the basement level. There were a few steps down to enter her apartment. Wawa was behind me, and I had forgotten that Wawa was a lot taller than me. His head suffered a hit on the doorway beam. He had to duck under the beam to get into the room then he was able to stand up. Our family did not have that problem only because we were short. Besides, the ceiling was lower in the basement than the rest of the house. Sorry about that, Hunny! He just rubbed his head with a smile. What was in his mind? He may as well have fallen down the mountain and still smile.

As soon as we walked in, I immediately recognized the same couch that Vavó and I sat in as we watched the Stooges years ago when I was in middle school!

My eyes found Andy and Henry on that couch. Wawa stood the closest to the couch, and Andy slowly moved his head up to look at him. Wawa's height frightened Andy so much that he screamed, "Mommy, they are here!"

Andy would not dare to get off the couch. Joey was not home yet. He was busy with his work at the Boys & Girls Club. Mommy walked over to us and met Wawa. Wawa spoiled her with a bouquet of flowers, and I could tell Mommy enjoyed the flowers immensely. Wawa met Grandma next. Then we put away our travel bags in the other room where we had planned to sleep overnight. I urged Wawa to follow me. I wanted him to meet Vavó. Off we went upstairs to Vavós place. This time I warned him to be careful not to hit his head again!

My beautiful Vavo′was dazzled by Wawa's looks! She spoke this word repeatedly in Portuguese, "Bonito" which means handsome. I interpreted for Wawa, and once Wawa learned what that word meant, he beamed with his dazzling smile.

Remember I explained how much Vavó loved to go big with Christmas traditions. In her Christmas spirit, she encouraged us to feast on her sampler platter filled with sweets. Vavó and Wawa enjoyed each other 's company, and I think Vavó even flirted with him. Oy Vey! Still, I cherished those moments of them together.

I believe with all myheart that she loved him. Maybe just not Vavó, my Mommy and Grandma did, too!

At last, my younger brothers warmed up to Wawa. While Mommy cooked dinner, we watched a movie. I snuck out to inform Mommy that Wawa cannot have pork because he was Jewish. Dinner had chorizo, and it was in everything Mommy had made for dinner. Mommy felt terrible, and I assured her that there was no need to feel bad. After all, she just met Wawa! Mommy whipped up a Hamburger Helper meal for him. Wawa saw what had gone on, and I apologized to him. He urged me not to worry, and he enjoyed his meal with us.

After dinner, we visited my uncle at my Grandma's place on the top floor of the house. My Uncle Aiden often sat in his favorite wooden rocking chair, and that was exactly where we found him. He was a brother of my favorite uncle, Dylan, who was in prison at the time. Wawa endured Aiden's kazillion questions! Perhaps he wanted to check Wawa out and see if he earned my uncle's stamp of approval.

Aiden's and my Grandma's smoking started to fill up the air. Grandma sensed that Wawa was not comfortable being in the smoking environment and got up from the couch to open windows. As a gentleman, Wawa politely said that it was ok. I thought to myself, "No, it was not, stop being so darn polite!"

Before we knew it, my Uncle Aiden welcomed Wawa to the family! They shook hands, and it was his way to inform me that I got his blessing. I was flabbergasted! I was not sure how my adoptive family would react since I got beaten up over a Black guy. Make no mistake - Wawa is clearly a Black guy! Obviously, a lot has changed since I left for a foster home. Clearly, they were ok with that, but not with my brothers' father.

Joey finally arrived home from work. We spent the night in his apartment which gave us more time with him. We jammed to the music, played games, opened gifts, and chatted merrily. The next day we woke up to see snow outside. Snow began to come down heavier, and that caused a concern. We were worried about the dangers being on snowy roads on our drive back to D.C. Our decision was made to cut the trip short and informed my family. They understood. We wanted to tell Vavó of our decision; so, we walked down to Vavó's place. You know, I never got to speak Portuguese fluently. Still, Vavó understood me enough through our "baby talk," and she tried to bribe us with food to stay longer. I had to convince her to let us go because of the dangerous weather, and she finally released her grips on us. As sadness registered on her face, she made sure to let us know that she was elated of our visit and ended her conversation toward Wawa with this word, "Bonito." Did that make you smile?

It did for me. We quickly gathered our things and put them in our rental car. Then we hit the road back to D.C. The drive was over 7 hours; so, we had plenty of time on the road to talk about our trip. Wawa shared his reflection that he felt honored by my uncle's acceptance of him and brought him into my adoptive family. As for my reflection, I thought what would have happened if daddy was still in the picture. I think the outcome of the trip would probably have ended differently. Besides, I would have never allowed Wawa to meet daddy. I was relieved that daddy was cut out of the family.

Wawa and I got invited to a friend's house for a New Year's Eve party in D.C. We knew most people there through Gallaudet Dance Company. It was like a family reunion. Such a nice and relaxing visit! At the time, I had a pager called WyndTel. It was designed specifically for Deaf and Hard of Hearing people to share texts. Mine went off constantly with a vibration that felt like buzzing. When I finally checked my pager, I had received a message that my favorite Vavó had gone to the hospital and might not make it. I broke down into tears, and Wawa came up to me to ask what was wrong. I was too upset to talk. I handed him my pager for him to read the message himself. Just a few days ago, Vavó begged for us to stay and spend more time with her. I often wondered if she knew that her time was up soon. She was always a strong woman on the move and did not show any sign of illness. Later, we found out what had happened to her.

Vavó had a family member who always stayed connected with her to check in on her especially during the holiday season. Whenever the family member called her, Vavó faithfully picked up the phone and talked for a while. But not this time! Calls to Vavó's went unanswered, and the family member decided to take a drive to check on her just to be cautious. Vavó was found on her couch. The same couch where we watched the *Three Stooges*, where she taught how to sew, and where we celebrated holidays. A 911 call was made, and she was taken to a hospital. We were all shocked and did not expect that at all.

We booked a rental car the next day and got ready to head out. Wawa changed into a black suit, and I asked why in the world was he dressed like that? Vavó was at the hospital, not at the funeral home. He said he was aware of where she was at and just wanted to pay respect in that way. Boy, I was not happy with him. Let it be known that he was the only one overly dressed. When we arrived at the hospital, we found her hooked on a respirator machine. Grandma was not ready to let her go, and her sister-in-law was there to offer her support. Mommy was with us in the room, and we all barely talked with each other. It was heartbreaking to see how hard it had been for Grandma, she hugged and pleaded for Vavó to wake up.

The truth is Vavó was not really in her body. Her body basically was laid down on the bed, and it made no response, not even with Grandma's appeals. In fact, she did not even breathe on her own. Only the oxygen machine did that. I asked everyone to leave the room so I could have alone time with Vavó. Everyone left then I walked up to the right side of her bed to look at her face.

Her face was so beautiful, as the ray of sunshine shone on her. I got closer to her then hugged her as my tears dripped down my face. I thanked her for being a huge part of my life, for loving me, for teaching me things, and always made it work out with our communication. I was so grateful she did not let my deafness or language barrier stop us from being close to each other. All of this felt so surreal. I will always carry her traditions with me. Few days later, Vavó had gone home to be with Jesus. I made the decision not to attend her funeral service because I had my peace with her in that hospital room. It is my belief that Vavó had her celebration when she arrived in Heaven. She danced with Jesus, dripped her grilled cheese in her coffee, and celebrated!

Mommy and I used AIM to communicate with each other. At the time, I still lived in D.C. Through that mode, she shared with me about my favorite Uncle Dylan's passing. He died in prison. I was upset and thought he was taken too soon! Besides, he was supposed to get out of prison soon and be on his way home. I guess God had another plan for him.

God's timing is always a mystery. Grandma mailed the letters that Uncle Dylan had written to me but for some reason, they were never sent out to me. He got my last letter, but it was never opened before his passing. I would like to believe that he is in a better place now than in prison. Still, I will never forget how he protected me and supported me. He would have taken the bullet for me. I cherish my sweet memories of my visits with him. He had love for chocolate like I do now. He had me get his favorite candy, Reese Cups, from the vending machine every time I visited him in prison. Now I think of him when I eat Reese Cups just as I think of Vavó when I eat the silver wrapped Hershey Kisses.

Chapter 11

Now What?!?

Remember that Union Station where Wawa and I had our first date? I worked there at a diner called Johnny Rocket. I loved my coworkers. Most of them were from other countries internationally, and I always learned something new from them. Even there were hilarious moments that caused me to laugh hard enough to almost pee in my pants. I never had a dull moment.

My goodness, I loved their food, their shakes, and of course, their mini jukeboxes! That meant music! I am all about music! Who does not like the good old Oldies music? The jukeboxes sat on the customers' tables, and we gave them a nickel for them to play a song. Most people chose songs such as *Under the Boardwalk* by the Drifters, *The Letter* by the Box Tops, and *Oh, Pretty Woman* by Roy Orbison. The only thing we did not have was roller skates. We could have skated around with the customers' orders like the old days.

Union Station is a place where people come from near and afar. It has Amtrak, cab service, and more. We saw all kinds of people come in and out - students on field trips, tourists, and commuters. The same goes for all races and sizes. Here is a story I can laugh about now that I did not back then - A couple in their 60's came to the diner, and I was their waitress. They got glasses of water, and I took their orders. They wanted fries and sandwiches. Fries were ready first, so I brought it out and placed it in the center of their table. I took a step back to look at the couple. They looked so cute, and they held hands. As I admired them, I took a deep breath then exhaled only to have something fly out of my nose! That something landed right in the middle of their table. I did not know what to do! I felt panicked and glanced at the couple. The wife calmly took a napkin and wiped it off the table. She literally saved me from embarrassment!!! I ran to the back of the restaurant and told my boss what had just happened then. He was shocked and laughed his head off! Amazingly they still gave me tips! God bless that couple for He knew who they were.

My birthday month, February, arrived! Wawa got me flowers and a card. Then a few days later, we went out for a Valentine's dinner, but it did not feel like a celebration. Lately I noticed something was off about Wawa. He did not text as often as before, and my vibes told me that something was up. As soon as I got off from work and waited for the metro bus to arrive, I decided to text him to ask if he was alright. He texted back and said that he wanted to talk to me in person. It was already late at night, and I could not meet him until another day. I did not want to wait any longer to find out. I told him to go ahead and text to tell me what was on his mind. In the next few minutes, he shared this. He felt that I was still young and should take advantage of this time to explore life more. He did not want us to settle down and get serious right away. In other words, he did not want to rob me of my opportunities.

It was hard for me to swallow after I saw his texts. My heart was hurt. I felt as if he rejected me. I was madder with the fact that he decided to wait to tell me AFTER my birthday and Valentine's Day. Do you not think that we both could have saved money on those foolish Valentine gifts if he was going to break my heart afterward? Thank you, Hallmark and Godiva. Hope you guys enjoyed the profits. Yes, I am known for being sarcastic. OY VEY! Perhaps he wanted to wait to do it at the right time. He truly did love me and with selfless love, he let me go. I did not know how long this break up would last. Would we ever go back together or was it really the end of our relationship? Only God knew then.

I stayed busy with work, school, and even learned more about my family life. I decided to apply for the position as Residential Night Assistant at Model Secondary School for the Deaf in D.C. and got the job. I enjoyed my work with coworkers and deaf teenage girls. After a few months of working there, my manager approached me to see if I would be interested in another position to work in Enhancing Student Success Program which oversaw suspensions and discipline programs that offered teachers strategies for classroom behavior management. I accepted and felt honored to be trusted to work with students and let them know they were not alone in their struggles. They did not like the community services, but in the end, they always felt good about themselves. I was forever thankful for this opportunity. In fact, this experience reminded me of the time I volunteered at Timothy Youth Summer Camp in Brockton, Massachusetts and of my home.

Five months have passed since my breakup with Wawa. During that phase, Wawa and I stayed civil and kept in touch with each other. Though it was not an easy thing to do! I tried to respect his space. Sometimes we ran into each other in the commuter lodge and made small chats, then continued with our lives separately. Still, I could not take him out of my mind. There was something special about this guy. I prayed to God that He would grant me the patience and willingness to wait for him for however long. Then when I least expected it, Wawa texted me!

He wanted to know if I would like to go out for dinner at UNO's with him. I told him that I would love to. I had to remind myself that it was NOT A DATE. Just like friends going out for dinner. I pushed my emotions away and tried to enjoy our time together as friends. That night we met at Union Station and walked over to UNO's. I remember the host seated us on the second-floor balcony. The waiter took care of our orders and drinks. While we waited, we caught up on what was news with our lives. Even after the meals arrived at our table, we talked and laughed together. We never really ran out of something to say. He waited for the right moment to talk about some serious stuff. Always a gentleman, he waited until we both were done with our meals to start a different kind of conversation. Thank you, Wawa. I like to be able to enjoy my meals as well. Wawa pushed his plates aside and leaned forward over the table to look at my eyes. He shared his observations of my life. He noticed the changes in my life in these past few months about me being more stable with my education studies, in my working world, and in my personal life. Before I go on about that night, I wanted to share about my housing situation.

I moved into a different apartment near Howard University with a new roommate. Before the move, my living arrangement was interesting. I lived in an apartment that was located behind Gallaudet University's campus on West Virginia Avenue. As a student at Gallaudet, the walk to the apartment was short. When I needed to go to work, I used the metro bus service. The bus stopped at Florida Avenue and West Virginia Avenue. Usually, my shift at Johnny Rockets ended late at night, and that made me more alert of my surroundings as I walked home. At that stop it was not a safe place to be alone, and many times I walked past a few prostitutes who waited on the side of the street for pickups.

As soon as I got into my apartment, I went straight to my bedroom. Mind you, it was not an ordinary bedroom nor anywhere inside the one-bedroom apartment. I turned a patio sunroom into my bedroom. It had a privacy screen but did not have the luxury of warmth. I sacrificed my space to give my roommate and her boyfriend the privacy they needed, and I wanted my own room. I figured this was better than nothing. Yes, I slept on the deck even in the winter season. Now that I look back, I could have put up the plywood boards to construct a room somewhat. There was no need for air conditioning during the summertime. After all, I had gotten a nice breeze at night. Wawa did visit me there a few times, and he was in disbelief that I could sleep there comfortably.

It was time for a change. I thought it was best for me to move to an apartment near Howard University with an older Christian roommate, even though I did have my own bedroom that kept me warm during the winter. Wawa was thrilled that I moved out of the 'ice cube' room. Still, I had to deal with different issues with my new place. He wanted to stop by to visit me, and this was before our breakup. When I flicked on the light switch as soon as we walked into the apartment, a bunch of cockroaches scattered on the wall to escape into darkness. I was so proud to show this place to my boyfriend. He froze and blinked his eyes. Yup. He just saw that. Hey, the rent was cheap! Besides, it was better than nothing. It's got a roof over my head, and I've got my own room. I think I was good with that.

Back to that night at UNO's, Wawa and I continued our discussion about the changes in my life. I worked on my relationship with Mommy and my biological brother, Patrick. Patrick even came out to D.C. to visit me and stayed with me at that place near Howard University. I only have one memory of Patrick and me from when I was a little girl. He visited and brought over a bowl of goldfish. Two days later, the fish died. I have bad luck with fish. That is why I do not do fishkeeping.

Back to the subject of Patrick, I was in Massachusetts for my Uncle Dylan's funeral. Dylan was one of the person's who would protect me, and one of the ways he did that was he told Mommy that her boyfriend had hurt me. He even displayed how I was hurt. She just told him to get over it, and that it was nothing. Dylan did all he could to protect me. I decided to go to the funeral to pay my respect. We went back to Grandma's house after the funeral service. Uncle Aiden was at his usual spot in the rocking chair, and I was in Mommy's apartment to help with the dishes to keep myself busy. Things turned strange in the next few minutes.

My brother, Andy, walked into the apartment with my brother, Patrick, and his girlfriend. I was surprised to see Patrick! After all these years, it took Uncle Dylan's death for us to finally meet each other. Patrick was close with Dylan. To refresh your mind, Patrick was the second child in my biological family, and I was the baby. Patrick and I shared an older brother, Richard. Richard was in fact Dylan's best friend. How bizarre was it that my adoptive brothers, Andy and Henry, played with Patrick's girlfriend's boys.

They only knew Patrick by his birth name, not by the nickname that my adoptive family called him. No one else outside of the family used his nickname. I did not know how they made the connection that Patrick was my biological brother. We both waved awkwardly at each other, and Alan led them to my Grandma's house so that they could pay their respect. I was still in my Mommy's house trying to understand what had just happened here. When Mommy came home from the store, I told her who was at Grandma's house. She was surprised, too. We both went up to Grandma's together. Patrick sat on one end of the couch while I sat on the other end. He at times looked at me. We did not talk but listened to others' conversation. As usual, I pretended I understood the conversations and nodded my head.

Eventually, Patrick and his girlfriend were ready to leave. We all said goodbyes. I digested all that just had happened earlier. The next day, Patrick called Mommy, she searched for me and found me in another room. She held her white landline telephone by her ear and as she pointed to the phone, she mouthed, "Your brother on the phone." Patrick had some questions for me, and Mommy played the role of interpreter for us. He wanted to know when I was scheduled to go back to D.C., and I told him my plan was to leave in two days. He wanted me to come over the very next day for lunch and for us to get to know each other. I was fine with that. Truthfully, I was nervous because I did not know what to make of this visit. I prayed for God's protection and for peace in our time together.

Our visit went well. We got to know each other, had lunch, and took some pictures together. This visit took place in 2000. It means we had a disposable camera, and the quality of pictures from that did not always come out great. It is as if we played with a lottery only to hope we strike it out that our photos will come out great after we paid for them to be developed. Today, the kids got it easy. One click then view the picture whether to keep or delete it all in less than a minute right on their phone!

Patrick told me a little bit about my biological father. He did not like him. He told me that our mom and my father always fought. One time we were in the back seat of the car, they would fight, and Patrick would hold me close to protect me. I do not think he was aware at the timet hat I was Deaf and could not hear them screaming and fighting. He did what he thought was the right thing to do.

I knew it would take more than just a day for Patrick and me to catch up and fill in the gap of all those missing years. The experience made it more precious that we shared that day together. I left the next day and rode on the Peter Pan bus back to D.C. My life continued with school and work at M.S.S.D. I worked on an overnight shift one evening when Patrick contacted me through AIM to let me know that he was on a train to visit me! Goodness! Bro, thanks for the head up! I could see that he wanted to spend more time with me and explore D.C. It did not matter that I had no sleep after the shift. I was so excited that finally a family member came to visit me.

After my shift ended, I went to Union Station and waited for my brother 's arrival. I still remember he arrived with two shopping bags filled with his personal belongings. We hugged then headed out to take the metro bus to my apartment. My brother was nervous while riding on the bus. He was not used to it and even tried to protect me. I laughed heartily and told him not to worry. He did not like that I laughed at him. Sorry, I didn't mean to tease you, brother.

After our arrival at my apartment, I introduced him to my roommate, and we all had a small chit chat before she left to do her errands. Patrick and I talked and talked into the evening! I wanted him to explore D.C.

beside Union Station, he had been to the Monument and a few other places. I took him to Adams Morgan to play a game of pool with my other "brother" who I went to Puerto Rico with. They both met and hit it off immediately. It seemed like they were best friends already. Their personalities are the same, and they both loved to give me a hard time. I guess that is what brothers do, right? The place was about to close, so we took the metro bus back to my place. Yes, he was nervous again on the bus. My other "brother" went on his way home. When we arrived at my place, we gabbed for hours. Keep in mind that I still had not gotten any sleep after my overnight shift. I think God gave me the extra energy to keep up with my brother.

Patrick shared some more about his upbringing. His story broke my heart for him. Some of us were not as lucky.

When our mother passed away, he was already a teenager. No one was interested in taking him in. Many foster parents or families who want to adopt prefer younger children or babies. For that reason, he lived in several foster homes until he aged out of the foster program. He was on his own now that he was an adult.

I asked him why he was not around when we were younger. He gave me his version of the visit he had with me when he brought over the goldfish. At the time, I was so young and did not understand the situation.

I do remember I rode my pink bike as he talked with Mommy. At that time, Mommy, Joey, and I moved into Vavó's apartment. At some point during Patrick's other visit with me, I told him not to visit me ever again. He never visited again. I was shocked when he told me that. I didn't even remember saying that to him. I could not believe that he stayed away from me for such a long time. I cannot imagine how he felt at that moment. For him to be in twenty-seven different foster homes then heard his little sister said to stay away, he felt lost and confused. Compared to my experience, I was blessed to deal with only two foster homes, and one of them was not a great experience. I know that not all foster homes are nice.

I apologized to Patrick. It was never my intention to hurt him or dismiss him like that. I was too young to fully understand the whole situation. We both agreed not to allow this to happen again with us not being in touch with each other for years.

As Wawa listened, he saw the difference in me that I no longer carried burdens on my shoulder and that I had made new changes in my life like a new job. We talked a bit more then he asked if I would like to give our relationship another try. I was surprised and asked him to repeat the question! I wanted to make sure I understood him clearly and correctly! Again, he asked the same question. I was thrilled and of course, I told him YES! The ladies who sat at the table next to us clapped hands and smiled at us. They probably thought I said yes to his marriage proposal. But that did not matter. All that mattered to me was that he still wanted to be in this relationship with this crazy lady, ME. I did not know who was crazier, Wawa or me.

We obviously missed each other so much and tried to stay strong when we were apart. It was not easy. There were some guys who wanted to date me, but I was not interested. Ladies wanted to date this hot dude, and I do not blame them. We were not interested in dating others. Praise the Lord! It was great to be back in his arms again. I did sometimes wonder why he did not date other ladies who were closer to his age or smarter. ONLY GOD KNOWS. There was no way I would let Satan feed me lies that I was not good enough for Wawa. I felt thankful and blessed.

It was a bit of a challenge trying to juggle school and work. I worked an overnight shift, and that meant no sleep. It had begun to affect my ability to do well in school. I decided it was best for me to leave my job at M.S.S.D and focus more on my college courses. I did love that job a lot, though I still had the job at Johnny Rockets. After all, I was able to do my assignments in the evenings and have my beauty sleep, too! Even if that meant I earned less money now. Sometimes in life I just must make the hard decision and accept the fact that I could not do it all.

Only God can. On the bright side, I was thankful that Wawa was still with me.

Three years passed…and I still had Wawa in my life! We made a major decision to live together. I was excited and nervous about this new chapter of my life. Nervousness started to take over, and I sent Wawa a text that I think I made a mistake and explained my concern. I felt I disobeyed God by living with a boyfriend before marriage. I said it again in person to his face. He looked at me and said, "If you want to change and drop this whole thing, please do let me know." This did not make me feel any better. I felt guilty and bad because this happened TWO days before our move in date. I started to feel panic then stopped to pray to ask God for his forgiveness for I had sinned against Him. Finally, I had the courage to tell Wawa that I had decided to stick with the plan and move in with him. Our home was at a beautiful apartment near the Waterfront D.C.

After I got over my guilt, I grew more excited. This was a whole new experience for me to live with a guy and try to compromise with his ways and my ways into our ways. We went out to shop for kitchen supplies, and when we returned from the shopping, Wawa was the one who put things away in the kitchen. I did not like how he had set things up in the kitchen! I rearranged them then we argued. Now that I look back, I had to laugh about it. There were other things in life that were worthy more to fight for than to argue about where pots and pans belong in the kitchen. Yikes. Thankfully, Wawa was very patient with me and took the time to listen. I would like to believe that deep down he understood why I behaved that way.

The location of our apartment was so convenient to the public transportation and within walking distance to cool spots such as Municipal Fish Market at The Wharf, Arena Stage, Zanzibar, Southeastern University, Smithsonian American Art Museum and so much more. It was the perfect spot with a great rental rate. At certain times, especially the 4th of July, we got an awesome view of fireworks. We had created many wonderful memories there with friends and family.

Chapter 12

I Do or I Don't

Back in the beginning of dating, we already had our up and down moments after 6 months of dating. We had so much to learn about each other, and religion was one of the topics. He is Jewish, and I am Christian. One day I asked him about his thoughts of our different religions and holiday celebrations. He told me the girls in his previous relationships never asked him about that or even bothered to ask. I shared that I felt it was important to know and have a better understanding of where our relationship stood on that topic. We then agreed that if we show respect to one another that all would be fine. Or will it? Only the good Lord knows.

Six months turned to a year, then two years, then three years. No wedding bells or a ring on my finger yet. The more we learned about each other, our relationship got better. Wawa still worked at Gallaudet University, and I left my job at Johnny Rocket. I started a new job at the Express Department Store at Pentagon City Mall. I was the only Deaf employee there, and the experience was quite interesting. The challenging part of the job was the staff meetings. I must give credit to my store manager who did try to get an interpreter. Yet, there were times when there were no interpreters. Their efforts to include me in the meetings involved notes and closed captions on the videos. Oftentimes I felt like I was a statue in a chair. I understood nothing. However, it was easier if it was just a one-on-one conversation. They did not know what or how to use me in the store.

They decided to put me in front of the store to be a greeter to customers. I must admit it felt like being a robotic greeter when I had to say the same greeting every time a customer comes in, “Hello, welcome to Express. Here’s the discount and the clearance, have a great time shopping.” It got to be very tiring. Though I loved the clothes there, and as a worker there I got great discounts. Yea!

I later learned that the store had a point system where it showed which worker sold the most to earn rewards points. One day as a greeter, I noticed a couple ladies who looked like they were from another country. I could tell by their body language that they needed help but was not sure who to ask for help. So, I approached them. Through my hand gestures, I asked if they were ok. They seemed relieved that I came up to them, and they communicated with hand gestures, too. They just wanted one of the workers to give them honest feedback on the clothes that they tried on; whether it looked great on them or not and to share feedback. I helped them out with different clothes in a variety of colors and pitched ideas. The ladies were happy and walked out of the store with confidence. I won the most reward points that day! My manager was surprised that I could do this. I knew I could do more than just being a greeter. The people who worked there were a great team. But they did need to be educated more about the needs of accessibility for employees with disabilities and give them more opportunities to expand their skills.

Soon I had decided that I did not want to stay on as a greeter at the job and left to look for another job. I had applied at the Family Service Foundation in Maryland and got the job. It came with huge responsibilities. I had to learn about medicines and types of disabilities. Then I had to take a test to pass in order to be able to administer medicines. I was grateful to be part of an amazing team, and the absolute best part of the job was that we ALL signed!

Clients were mostly Deaf; so, communication was wonderful. Each client had different disabilities, and some clients had blindness. I was able to get to know each client about their likes, dislikes, and hobbies. One client loved music and its vibrations. We made it possible to take him to meet with Gallaudet Dance Company. He was so happy. I remember the smile on his face, and how he jammed to the music. There was another client that I remember fondly. She was Deaf and blind, but that did not stop her from being a mother hen. She always checked to make sure everyone was ok, and even fixed anyone's shirt that was out of its place. It was impossible to not love her.

One of my coworkers was surprised to see me at this type of work. I was puzzled by that response and asked this person to explain why. This person said, "You are too pretty for this kind of job. You would not last more than a month here!" Glad to report that I proved this person wrong and I did work there for more than one month. More like for several months, even though I had a challenge with the transportation issue. At the time, I did not have a car, and my night shift hours were from 3 PM to 11 PM. By the time I got off, I had no one to take me to the metro train, and the metro train was already closed for the night. I ended up sleeping there overnight. I rarely got to see Wawa because he worked at Gallaudet during the day, and I tried to get home to nap before I returned to my job. It was as if days became a repeat. Wawa and I managed to have time together when I had my days off during my days off during the weekdays and some weekends.

Word of mouth is a terrific way to gather information. I spoke with some of my peers at work who also worked at another place called National Children's Center. I asked all kinds of questions about their work there. After I prayed about it, I thought it would not hurt if

I had applied for a job at the National Children's Center. I was blessed to get the job! I closed my chapter with the previous job. Immediately I experienced all the bonuses that the new job gave me - being closer to my home, easy transportation, and the best part of it, I was able to see Wawa more often!

My experience with the National Children's Center was different. I worked with a small group of men who were considered high functioning clients with a variety of disabilities. Each one of them was unique and had their own skill. Not all of them were Deaf. Most of them were able to do laundry, set the table, vacuum, make up their bed and so forth. I prepared dinner for them. Just like any other job, I am again forever thankful for that experience and to collaborate with a wonderful team because this was not an easy job. With these clients, there were never dull moments. Sometimes I wonder if they knew me more than I knew myself.

When I was at Family Service Foundation, my coworkers introduced me to television shows called The Bachelor and The Bachelorette. I got addicted to the shows! Being in a relationship and had started to think about marriage, I started to buy the Bride magazines. Before you go off on me, yes, I know! But I like to be prepared! I figured it was better to start research and prepare for the wedding. Ya never know!

Part of my work at the National Children's Center was to take clients out for excursions anywhere they want to go. Of course, it took some planning and budget to make this happen for them. One of their outings was at my place for a fellowship lunch and dessert. I was off for that event. They met Wawa, and he was so sweet with each of them. He took his time to talk with them. Some of us played games while others watched shows on TV or just simply listened to music. Afterwards, they returned home. One of the clients asked us to do this again. They really enjoyed themselves, and I was happy for them. Fun does not have to be at places that cost money. They needed to do something more than just stay inside the house all the time. I was glad they did not do that when I worked there. I took on more training for the job and continued to enjoy my job. I loved being closer to my home.

Wawa and I had some discussions about marriage. It had already been three years and still, nothing. I did not know when he was going to ask the question or anything. Then one day in August, I was off from work and flipped through TV channels. Then I saw this show on TLC called A Wedding Story. Proposal was not a traditional type where the guy asks the girl the question. It was different. That planted an idea in my mind. Ya know what? That was exactly what I was going to do. I got the ring that Wawa had planned to wear for the wedding and planned out the details right then. I put on my red evening gown, got the rose and ring. I had already posted a note on our apartment door that told Wawa to meet me at the waterfront. Here I was at the waterfront on a very hot summer day.

In the meantime, it was a very busy month for Wawa. He worked as an Academic Administrator at Gallaudet University, and at times he had to work longer hours than normal. When he finally got to our apartment and saw the note, he walked over to the waterfront to meet me. While I waited for him, there was a guy who came up to me and said he was available to date me. “Sorry, it is reserved,” I said to that guy. The red rose got baked under the sun, and it withered slowly. That was where I originally put the ring in then changed my mind. I did not want to take the risk of the ring being rolled into the river. Remember how I like to be prepared? I came up with a plan B which was to attach the ring to my high heel strap, and my evening gown hid the shoes. Wawa would not have known the ring was there!

I do not remember how long I stood there and waited for Wawa’s arrival. I stood in front of the Titanic Memorial Statue. It is still there if you want to Google it. The statue is of a man whose arms are stretched out. I thought of Celine Dion’s song, “My Heart Will Go On.” While we were together, he traveled frequently for work or for performance, and I often worked at odd hours. Our lives were busy, but we made it work by the grace of God.

The sky had gotten darker, and the streetlights came on. Tourists had left. My eyes caught Wawa afar. He walked up toward me with his head down to look at his phone to answer texts. When he got closer, he looked up and suddenly walked slowly. His face looked puzzled and was surprised to see me all dolled up.

We hugged and instead of doing all the talking, I gave Wawa a card with my writing in it. He read the card, and I bent down to take the ring off the strap. Then I got on my knee to ask him to marry me. Yup, I did that. I was a nervous wreck! I should have waited and let Wawa do that. Wawa read the card with a smile and happily accepted my proposal. The following Sunday we were at Wild Zappers and National Deaf Dance Theater rehearsal. After our rehearsal, Wawa called for a meeting then shared, "Guys, I want to let you know that Kimmy and I are not together anymore." Wawa and I saw their facial expressions as if they were confused. Then Wawa said, "Because we are engaged!" They were thrilled and ran over to me to see the ring. "Nope," I said, "The ring is on Wawa's hand!" They all took a U-turn to see his ring. It was really funny to see them do that! Admittedly, it felt strange. I proposed. Now what? We officially started with the wedding plans.

Four months later, it was Wawa's birthday. He decided to take the day off from work. I thought, "Oh, no!" I knew then to contact his coworker to let her know that the birthday guy was not coming in. You see, they have this tradition where each worker is responsible for the next birthday person's cake and celebration. She already contacted me to get the dibs on Wawa's favorite cake and such. You can imagine that she already got the cake, and this dude decided not to show up. I felt bad. I guess it did not bother him much.

I still had to go to work that day. When I got home that evening, I found Wawa on the futon watching his show. I went straight ahead to our bedroom to drop off my things. I noticed there was a golden box on the bed. I picked it up and brought it into the living room. I questioned Wawa about it. He playfully said that he knew nothing about it and to open it up. I told him that if this was what I thought it was then I would refuse to open it. He looked at me and asked, "Why not?" I said, "I would like to experience the proposal, too." He got up from the futon and turned off the TV. Then walked up to me on bended knee and asked the question. I answered, "Sorry I cannot give you the answer," and then I walked away. I was obviously joking, but that just ruined the mood! You could say we BOTH got officially engaged. Wawa took off his ring to wear it again on the wedding day and to allow me to get the attention with my engagement ring. I did not care since I was very down to earth and very easy to please.

We were still busy with dance rehearsals. Then in May, it was one of the dancer's birthdays, and she invited me to hang out with her for the weekend. There was no way I could turn that down. Girls just wanna have fun. We went out to a country club and did many different line dances. As a dancer, I truly enjoyed that. Before we did that, we watched a dance performance. While I was seated, I could not sit still and felt uncomfortable. I thought to myself that I cannot be sick now. I am here to celebrate my girl's birthday. I made it through the show. After the show, we went out to grab something to eat. We ate our lunch then chilled at her house until it was time to hit country line dancing. The country dancing was fun, then we got back to her house. Poor birthday gal, I must have kept her up all night. I could not sleep. I did not feel well yet I was hungry again. I got up in the middle of the night to grab food. She asked, "Kimmy, are you pregnant?" Umm, I did not think of that. I took the pregnancy test, and it came out positive! I am thankful that the birthday girl and her mom were there to support me. Honestly, I was shocked. I did not expect this to happen until after the wedding. I did not know how to tell Wawa the news.

In less than 8 hours, I was to see him at a dance rehearsal on Sunday morning. I prayed fervently. I was scared that I was a disappointment to God that I did not wait until my big day. Before the birthday gal and I arrived at the rehearsal, I wanted to stop by the store to get something like a goody bag to let him know the news. When we finally arrived at the rehearsal, we did what we normally do to prepare for any upcoming shows. That meant workout! Even though I did not feel well, I did my best. At the end of the rehearsal, I grabbed Wawa aside and gave him the goody bag. Yup! See I just let the card and bag to do all the talking. That day I was SCARED!!!! I had no clue how he would react to the news. He grabbed the bag and slowly pulled out one item at a time. Each item was a different baby object. Then he gave me a look that asked, "What is this all about?" I signed extremely fast, "You're going to be a daddy!" then closed my eyes because I feared his reaction. He looked at me for confirmation and asked, "You're pregnant? " Yup! I cried and cried. I was so overwhelmed with emotions. We both went back inside the room.

I forgot how or what we said to others. Most congratulated us. One had the nerve to say, "How can you afford it?" Really, Fool?! Some people! Luckily, this friend who has known this person for a long time smacked him for me. It took months to get used to morning sickness. There were some smells I could not stand. My top cravings were hotdogs and Coca-Cola. Still, I was not able to hold anything down. After the first trimester, it had gotten better. I was able to enjoy my pregnancy. We decided that we wanted to know the gender of our first baby. We went to our sonogram appointment, and they told us it was a BOY! Wawa was elated that his last name will carry over to the next generation. I had so many things on my mind. I worried about what my family and friends thought of me. I needed to find a doctor. I needed to finish the wedding plans. What about my job? You get the point! I just wanted to pause everything and sleep!

In October, we had our wedding day! That morning was a bit chaotic. I focused so much on the bridal party and wanted to make sure their needs were met. I neglected myself. I did not really eat much. I had a Deaf Jewish man style my hair; the same guy who smacked Wawa for not telling him that we were an item. The stylist had to wait for me while I was in the bathroom with morning sickness. I made sure I ate something. Then my hair got all worked up.

The wedding was beautiful. We only invited close friends and family since it was impossible to invite the whole world. So many people know Wawa. I only wish that my God Parents, Joey, Andy, Henry, and Grandma had shown up, but they could not make it. I believe that my Mommy, Vavó, my uncles, and Wawa's grandparents were there watching us and dancing from Heaven. It was so nice to have our loved ones to celebrate our special day. We decided to postpone our honeymoon to another time.

Three months later, I started to have contractions and called my doctor. She told me to wait a bit, and that it may be a false alarm. But the pain was too much for me to bear!

The time between contractions got closer and closer. A friendly reminder to you, we lived in D.C. and did not have a car. It was late at night. We called 911, and the ambulance arrived. Wawa was so excited that he grabbed the whole apartment with him! I sat on the futon and tried to even out my breaths. When the ambulance arrived, they told me to put on the shoes. I was ready to walk out without shoes. It was a nice fast ride in that ambulance. When we arrived at the Washington Hospital, I saw my doctor in her chair fast asleep! Really! Then I understood that she must have had a long day. A nurse had to check me to make sure that I was really in labor; that it was not Braxton Hicks. I know for sure my body was in labor. I told the nurse that I needed to use the bathroom. As soon as I got up, my water broke, and I looked up to the nurse with a sarcastic response, "Any questions?"

The nurse had informed my doctor and put me in the room. But I was not dilated yet, so we had to wait. I tell you, when this boy was in my tummy, he could not make up his mind just like he is in his life of 17 years. He wants out, but he wants in. So, we had to wait for our son to finally come out. We waited for 26 hours. Literally more than a day! It snowed outside. I watched the sunrise AND sunset. He finally came out, but doctors rushed him to the neonatal intensive care unit. Wawa and I were able to visit our son. He was a strong boy. It was hard for me to go home and be away from my son. He was there for a week. A few days later he was finally able to come home. It has been a joy to see him grow up. With him, there is never a dull moment. He is already jamming to the music, and has his groove.

During the holidays, something was amiss. We both celebrated Christmas and Hanukkah. I do recall the time I set up the Christmas tree, and Wawa uttered, "Why don't we just burn the tree?" That caught me off guard. He joked about it but did not understand what all the fuss about the tree was. Wawa loved to help me with the set up and decorate the tree…NOT. Christmas was MY favorite holiday. Christmas holiday had brought me back to my childhood memories of my Mommy who always played Christmas music. She sang and jammed while she put the tree together. I must say it might be the only time that all of us, even daddy, got together to do this activity. We were a jolly family.

Back to that moment where something was amiss during our first Christmas with our new 11-month-old son! I did not like the idea that Wawa had attended Christmas Eve service just for my sake the year before then the year after that. I felt like I was a single mom, but I was not. I tried to be respectable of Wawa's Jewish culture and tried to learn about the customs and food dishes. I tried to cook Matzo ball soup. Wawa still to this day applauds me for making it. I take zero credit since I make it out of the package box. I cannot even make it from scratch. No, do not give me the credit. But I was willing to include his religious celebrations such as Hanukkah and Passover.

I had some thoughts for a while about our marriage. I spoke with someone who was very close with Wawa. I told this person that I wanted to divorce Wawa. Yes, I did. Of course, I did not tell Wawa at that time that I had thought of it. This person supported my decision and said that guys were dumb. I was surprised to hear that. I was torn because I knew I married him, and I should stay with him. Things started to go down for us. When it rains it pours or that is what it felt like to me. We almost lost our car and our home. We struggled to find a job, and it was one thing after another. Do not get me wrong, Wawa had never hurt me or said anything harsh. He had no idea that I had planned to leave him with our son. I spoke with my foster mother about my struggle. We talked and prayed for God's wisdom. Then, I finally had the courage to tell him what was on my mind. He was shocked that I wanted to leave him. We slept separately after this. I slept in the bedroom while Wawa slept in the living room. It had been the toughest journey for the both of us. Wawa tried to give me space even when he was angry, hurt, and darn well confused.

On Christmas Day, as we opened the gifts with our son, Wawa held him for a long time. Through his cries, he said, "This will be our last Christmas together." I tried to be strong and be tough, but it was so hard. I knew in my heart that he did not deserve to be treated like this, but I just did not know what to do next or why I felt this way. The next few weeks, we were being civil and kept our distance. We were busy with planning for our son's second birthday. We both could use a little distraction. Though I noticed I was late with my period, and I thought it was due to all the stress these past few weeks. I went to get tested, and it came out that I was pregnant again. Perfect timing! I had informed Wawa of the news. He was not sure what to say because I wanted to end our marriage. He simply asked me what I wanted to do about it. It was a totally opposite reaction from the first experience with a firstborn. I told him, "Of course, I would keep the baby." I knew I could not even bring myself to abort it. It is not what I believe in. A baby is innocent.

The way I answered Wawa was cold, and there was no warmth in our conversation. I just could not keep up with whatever that bothered me any longer. Off I went to my room. I opened my Bible and prayed for God's wisdom and guidance. I fought and tried to seek His answer. I felt my head spinning. Then BAM! The Bible literally slapped me with His truth. In 1 Corinthians 7:10- 16 (NIV), it says:

> To the married I give this command (not I, but the Lord): A wife must not separate from her husband. But if she does, she must remain

> unmarried or else be reconciled to her husband. And a husband must not divorce his wife. To the rest I say this (I, not the Lord): If any brother has a wife who is not a believer and she is willing to live with him, he must not divorce her. And if a woman has a husband who is not a believer and he is willing to live with her, she must not divorce him. For the unbelieving husband has been sanctified through his wife, and the unbelieving wife has been sanctified through her believing husband. Otherwise your children would be unclean, but as it is, they are holy. But if the unbeliever leaves, let it be so. The brother or the sister is not bound in such circumstances; God has called us to live in peace. How do you know, wife, whether you will save your husband? Or, how do you know, husband, whether you will save your wife?”

When I read that, I cried and surrendered. I knew I could not bring my family through this mess. After praying and asking God for His forgiveness, I had to ask another person for his forgiveness. I went to the living room and spoke with Wawa. I did not tell him about the verses. I told him that I would like to keep working on our marriage, and that I would not file for divorce. He was such a gentle man. He asked me if this is really what I wanted to do. He could have blown up or destroyed our apartment. He did none of that. He was very patient and loving. I do not know how in the world I ever deserved this man. He showed more of God's characteristics better than I did, that is for sure. We took our time to get to know each other all over again and rebuilt our relationship. I know it was Satan who tried so hard to destroy God's gift called Marriage.

Months went by, and our baby girl had arrived. My delivery with this girl was short and easy within 2 hours, unlike her big brother's. Thank you, daughter! About a year later, our friend came over to visit. We sat in the living room. She and I were having a Sister-in-Christ conversation. Wawa was in the room, too, and saw our conversation. I assumed that Wawa did not understand since he was not a Christian. Then Wawa smiled, "Oh, no, I get it. I am Christian. I am Messianic Jewish." I looked at my friend then back at him, "What?! When? Why didn't you tell me?" "Oh, I did not know I was supposed to tell you?" said Wawa. All of a sudden there were a lot of celebrations. I was happy for him. Poor Wawa, he was showered with many kinds of Bibles. My friend could not help herself. I was more like, "Yay, but I am going to keep an eye on you." I was not sure if it was just a phase for him or he said that to make me happy. I did not want that for him. I wanted him to decide that for himself, not for others. This was between him and God. I saw a beautiful transformation in him as months rolled by. He used to refuse to do any worship song that had "Jesus" in it. Then that Easter morning, he stood on the stage to praise him. I fell in love with Wawa all over again. So, Wawa and I had decided to celebrate our 5-year anniversary and went on a Deaf cruise for the first time. Thanks to my foster family for taking our kids under their wings. Few years later, the Lord blessed us with another child. My body was ready, but apparently this baby wanted to stay inside a bit longer. I had to walk around the hospital and Wawa told me "Come on, let's do jumping jacks!" Really? Soon after that our third baby came into the world, and we all were surprised that it was a girl!! God had created each of our children unique and special in their own way.

Chapter 13

I Am a D.O.R.K.

Throughout my life, God has brought so many wonderful people in my life to teach me about Jesus. I cannot name all on this page, but the following people, Mrs. Rosy, my foster Momma, and the youth group made a difference in my life. He is forever faithful. It may have taken 6 to 7 years to get an answer for each of my prayers about my abusive childhood, rape, family relationships, and marriage. It was always God's perfect timing. Proverbs 3:5-6 became my life verse. While I do not understand why my life or the horrendous incidents I had to endure, or the situations that I see among my loved ones, I do know that when I trust Him, He will set my life. He WILL take care of me. With that said, I have learned to have a merry heart beyond measure! What I had experienced was understandably enough to drag me down, yet I went beyond measure and chose to trust God! Right now, I'm a D.O.R.K. and that is just enough for me.

"And before the world was made, God decided to make us his own children through Jesus Christ. This was what God wanted, and it pleased him to do it. And this brings praise to God because of his wonderful grace. God gave that grace to us freely. He gave us that grace in Christ, the one he loves." Ephesians 1:5-6 (ERV)

At this point, you can see how my life journey may be a bit confusing and how my family tree is sort of broken down or has a missing branch. Well, God is so GOOD! As I write this on June 10th, I will meet my second cousin for the first time to learn more about my family. All this started as I googled to search for information regarding my birth mother's death, and so forth. When I clicked on my mother's name, I felt like the Lord had poured down my family history. I was surprised at how easy I got that information. I did Ancestry online about 10 years ago, and I got frustrated because I did not have much information. I did not know where or what to look for. And if I was honest, I was scared. I was scared that I might offend someone or hurt their feelings by looking for my family. After all, I got beaten once before for telling my cousin about being adopted.

I had another opportunity when I lived with my foster family. The social worker asked me if I wanted to know where my biological father was. I remember standing there thinking and looking at my foster mother and remembered how it felt with my adoptive mother. So, I told my social worker no. Then they closed the case. I often wondered about him and had questions I would have liked to ask him. Again, I did not want to hurt my foster family's feelings. I swept my family tree under the rug and moved on. Or at least I tried to. I never talked about my biological family until I was well into my adult age.

I know Patrick is alive since I am friends with his girlfriend on Facebook. I guess it is all about timing. God's timing, not mine! I did not want to keep going through his girlfriend to pass on any information, I would much rather communicate with him myself. I decided to search him up on Facebook and there he was. I found him with Lord's help, of course. It has been a few days that we have kept in touch. I told him we cannot do 'reconnection' every 20 years. We must keep in touch as often. My kids are his nieces and nephew. I want them to meet their uncle. Hopefully soon, we all will take a family trip to New England.

Why do I share these stories? What was the point? First, I am D.O.R.K.! I am proud of it, too. This may sound weird that I proudly proclaim that I am a DORK!!!! Seriously, I am the Daughter of a Risen King, and I am forever thankful for our wonderful Savior, my Heavenly Father, Jesus Christ. Yes, He loved me so much that He died on the cross for me. Guess what? He loves you, too and yes, He indeed died on the cross for you, too.

So, when you feel unworthy, imperfect, or crazy, don't! Because you are perfect in every step of the way! We must stop trying to measure up in earthly things or worry about what others think or say about us. Only thing that matters is what our Heavenly Father says of us. We are children of God. He created us and knew our names before we were even born. Can you say Amen? Amen! He never left us when our earthly father or mother did. He is always right beside you and waits for you to seek HIM. Deuteronomy 31:8 (NIV), in the Bible says, "The Lord himself goes before you and will be with you; he will never leave you nor forsake you. Do not be afraid; do not be discouraged." How awesome is this? We just need to trust him and let Him do his job, for He knows what He is doing.

On June 9, 2021, I sent a message to my auntie, who was married to my biological uncle, my birth mother's brother, on Facebook. I had hoped to find more information regarding my biological mother and my uncle. Few days went by, then weeks. I am not going to lie. I was a bit discouraged to not have heard back from her - I sort of felt like she did not want me to bother her. I was practically a "stranger" to her. I had always trained my kids not to speak with strangers. I guess that applies to a grown up as well. I wanted to meet and get to know my aunt. Then the moment I had waited for finally came on July 15, 2021. There was a Facebook message from her. My heart nearly stopped. It was a message from my auntie who married my uncle. Did you not see what I just wrote? My uncle who was my birth mother's brother! Unfortunately, my uncle passed away in 2018. I am truly glad that I have someone from my birth family's side that can tell me more about my mother and my uncle. And this is what my auntie said:

> "Hello Kimberly, I do not know where to start. Your uncle and I loved your mother. When she passed, we were devastated. Your uncle and I had no control on what happened to you and your brother, Patrick... I am sorry for your loss. I hope your life is a good life. Love Auntie."

I responded back to her and told her that I was grateful to hear from her. It meant the whole world to me. Through her messages, I learned that my mother, Betty, loved her children, her parents, and her only brother. She was a tough lady with a good heart. The family visit was always nice. Before Betty passed away at an early age, she complained about the pain in her back. I do not know why I had always thought she had passed away from a heart attack. This would make sense now, since if she had a heart attack, there would be no time for Betty to be able to talk with Sandra about taking care of us. She did say that my uncle would have loved to meet me. She hopes we will meet soon someday. I now have a photo of him. He looks like a jolly fella. Also got a beautiful picture of them on their wedding day! I started to create a family album and added the photos of my family members. I used to groan about family albums because I had very little information about my family. Now as I create it, I am in awe.

On the same day, I also responded to an email from a guy who claimed to be my second cousin, K.R. I wanted to ask him a few questions to confirm if we were indeed related to one another. He was one of the people who helped me with the ancestry online. I was at my son's track meet with my husband when I got a prompt response from K.R. I was surprised at how quickly he responded back. My emotions were high, and I did not know what to say, do, or even think! I passed my phone to my husband like it had cooties. My husband had this huge smile on his face and said, "Kimmy, you need to face this and find more information about your family. You can do this." Then he handed me the phone. Don't you hate it when someone else was right? I took my phone back.

I spent a lot of time in prayers and sought God's guidance. I had the courage to respond back to K.R. K.R. asked for more information about my family to make sure we both had the same information. He, too, was surprised that after all those years, we finally connected. We immediately exchanged our contact information. He had photos in his family tree that matched exactly with what I had already known. That resolved my concern about authenticity. I then knew this was not a scam. It would probably be different if I have no photos of any family member. If that was the case, it might take me a bit longer to respond since I am very cautious about these things.

Warren and I met my cousin for the first time through a video conference on Zoom with a sign language interpreter. I think we both were awestruck that we have finally met after all those 39 years. My cousin explained what my mother, Betty, was like back in the good old days. He also explained what happened after my mother's funeral. After her death, everything happened so fast that all her three kids disappeared. My brothers were gone, and I went to live with Sandy. We spoke for a good two hours. Of course, that was not enough. It was a lot for my mind to absorb all the new information! K.R. and I have been in touch since we met on the Zoom. Thank goodness for technology; otherwise, I would have to wait for snail mail, and by the time I receive them it would be old news.

The latest update I had gotten was when I traveled on my own to New England on September 16 to 18th, 2021. Let's just say that it was indeed worth the long trip. I went up to celebrate my childhood friend's 40th birthday! Not only that I also needed to find more information about my biological family. With the new added information, a lot of things started to make sense here and there. First, my brother, Richard, did not pass away at the age of fifteen; he was already an adult. He passed away at the age of eighteen from alcoholism. I found a picture of Richard with my favorite Uncle

Dylan. They looked well grown. I guess it was Grandma who tried her best to tell me what had happened to Richard. The age was off, but everything else was correct.

I decided to be brave enough to take the DNA test through Ancestry. The results came in, and it is quite interesting to see what my blood represents:

63% Portugal
43% Spain
8% Puerto Rico
4 % Northern Africa
3% Basque
2% in Senegal, Germanic Europe, Mali
1% in Cameroon, Congo & Western Bantu Peoples and European Jewish

Wow! But I know for fact I am 100% Daughter of the Risen King! Amen! Praise the Lord for that. It is like the Lord slowly puts the puzzle pieces together to make a beautiful masterpiece.

Time heals wounds. I finally let my guard down to those who are Veterans. I need to remind myself that not all of you are "BAD GUYS", and that there are GREAT HEROES out there. I just want to put my two cents in for those children. You cannot be a hero to our country if you cannot be a HERO in your own home, behind the closed door and those four walls. You may be a Hero for fighting for our country. But a real HERO begins with your own family. Be a great role model for your children so that they could be great Heroes because of your example. So today, I can say THANK YOU to a REAL HERO. You know who you are for being a great HERO. I am thankful to know that there are great Veterans out there.

A Soldier's Prayer

Lord, hold our troops in your loving hands. Protect them as they protect us. Bless them and their families for the selfless acts they perform for us in our time of need. We ask this in the name of Jesus, Christ our Lord, Amen.

Chapter 14

What's the Point?

As I had already mentioned a few times, Christmas is my favorite time of the year. I just love playing Christmas songs and putting up the decorations. How pretty it looks when you look out of your window and see the snowflakes falling. You get that a lot in New England, but not so much in Virginia unless we are lucky.

Bless my husband's heart. In October, most people get dressed up in costumes, go to a Fall Festival, go on a hayride, and then on the last day of October, people go out to do trick or treat in search of big candies. But not in our house, you really want to know what we do? I will tell you. We put up our Christmas tree. Yes, you just read this right. I put up a Christmas tree in the month of October about 99.9% of the time. I didn't do it in 2021. When the Christmas tree is set up, I always feel at home. It brings so many warm memories of the past and present and creates memories for the future. I am sure you might have already read or watched The Christmas Carol by Charles Dickens. It is about a scrooge who always says, “Bah, humbug,” a miser whose sole pursuit of financial success had left him a bitter and lonely old man. But The Scrooge got a few visits from a Ghosts of Christmas Past, Present and Future ultimately teaching him to open his heart to the spirit of Christmas and to find the joys of friendships and family before Christmas. So, let us talk about these three journeys from the Past, Present and the Future.

Let us take a trip to the Past…

"A cheerful heart is good medicine, but a crushed spirit dries up the bones." Proverbs 17:22 (NIV) The word, *merry*, is translated from the Hebrew word as "Be Glad" in Psalm 68:3 (NIV) "But may the righteous be glad and rejoice before God; may they be happy and joyful."

The word, medicine, from the verse is defined as cure or healing. A glad heart makes the body healthy. It does have a positive effect on our physical health. What are the other benefits of having a merry heart? Proverbs 15:13 (ESV) says, "A merry (glad, joyful) heart makes a cheerful countenance; but by sorrow of the heart the spirit is broken." Having a merry heart has a positive effect on our physical health, joy shows on our face, and opens the opportunity up to help others around us. The thoughts we hold in our hearts affect what we say, what we do, and how people see us. We can decide each day to have a merry heart by reading the abundant promises that God had given to us and that is through HIS WORDS - the Bible. Trust that what He said in the Bible is true. We have the power to change our thoughts. We take one thought at a time, line it up with what God says, and believe in HIS Words. Because our Heavenly Father provides for all the needs of HIS children and that is US, so we, too, can experience peace in our heart.

Biblically the HEART means the center of the personal life referring to the innermost part of one's mind. And our countenance is what shows on our faces. What goes on inside, shows outside. People may not be able to read our thoughts, but they often see what goes on by looking at our faces or hear what we say at the tone of our voices, or even the ways we sign, and observe our behaviors. When you get the joy in your heart it does not only benefit us, but it also benefits those around us. When people see that we are joyful and are in peace within ourselves then they would want what we have. Proverbs 15:14 (NIV) says, "The discerning heart seeks knowledge, but the mouth of a fool feeds on folly." Here is another one from Proverbs 15:30 (ESV) "The light of the eyes rejoices the heart, and good news refreshes the bones." So based on our own actions, the others would want to know more about you and may ask you questions. I had some people come up to me and ask how come I was always happy. My response always points to Jesus. If it wasn't from him, I would be a fool. Only through Him will I have joy and experience peace in my heart. He will indeed do the same for you, too.

I do understand that our lives are a mixture of sunshine and rain, mountains and valleys, births, and deaths. Should we only accept only good things from God and never bad things? We get mad at God when some things do not go the way we wanted. It is time to walk through everything God had destined for us and to do it with guts. You know how sometimes we convince ourselves that we are the only ones walking on earth who have ever ____? You fill in the blank. Been cheated on? Divorced? Betrayed? Been abused? Lost a child or a loved one? Barren? Orphaned? Raped? Drug or Alcohol addiction? Homeless? Jobless? The list can go on. We often make ourselves the center of the universe. God deals this with you and me every day, every hour, every minute, and even every second. So, no, we are not the only ones on the planet that experiences such heartache.

Let us look at some examples of women in the bible:

Sarah. She was the wife of Abraham. She was a woman of faith and was a great example to the Jews and Christians throughout the years. She had it all. She was beautiful, married to a rich and godly man, and even had servants. She bravely obeyed God's will for her life and traveled to a foreign but a promised land - and I know she was covered in swanky accessories while she did it. She was living the dream, and it sounds sexy! But let's take a closer look. You will see she was also a woman who had experienced such disappointment. Her perfect veneer of beauty, traveling and wealth was just that: a veneer. It concealed her heartbreak neatly beneath the surface. To dig a little deeper, we find out she suffered a lifetime of infertility which was a very big deal in ancient Middle Eastern Culture, when a woman's ability to have children and scads of them dictated her worth.

Sarah's heart desire was to have her empty arms filled, to love on a child, to nurse, to nurture and raise up a tiny human that she could call her own. Year after year went, desolate and dry. But Sarah, this exotic and noble woman, hid deep in her heart hope for the future. You see God had promised to make Abraham the father of a great nation. So, Sarah waited and waited for God to make good, but the years went by, and she grew incredibly old and quite discouraged. I am sure Sarah is ready to throw in the towel on this whole "Follow God to Canaan" and "you'll be the mother of a great nation" thing. In Genesis 16, Sarah tried to take the matter into her hands and manipulate the situation. She gave her servant Hagar to her husband, Abraham, in the hope to have a baby. So, let's look at Genesis 16:2 (NLT)

"So, Sarai said to Abram, "The Lord has prevented me from having children. Go and sleep with my servant.

Perhaps I can have children through her." And Abram agreed with Sarai's proposal."

Really, Dude? Abe, it does not seem like it took you very long to think about that decision. Just saying! Can you even imagine lending your husband, your soul mate, out for a night to your maidservant? I mean, what do you say to them? "Good luck, Boo!" Or "Please go to the farthest tent down!" or maybe you just plug your ears, close your eyes and say, "LALALALALA!" Well, this has happened. Hagar became pregnant, her relationship with Sarah, of course, became sketchy and brought about jealousy, contempt and fighting. I can only imagine how Sarah felt when she saw Hagar's belly grow bigger, witnessed Hagar's experience of childbirth, and possibly saw her breastfeed her baby. No matter how badly we thirst, it is never a good idea to try to take matters in our hands. We all are so much like Sarah, yearning for our hearts' desire - hoping, believing, waiting, getting frustrated with God's timing, and trying to fix whatever the situations are, on our own.

The next thing you know, the three strangers showed up at Abraham's tent. One of these men, "the angel of the Lord," asked him, "Where is your wife, Sarah?" Abraham answered, "She's in a tent." The angel told him, "I will return to you next year, your wife Sarah, will have a son!" During that conversation between the guys, the tent was a flexi wall so Sarah could hear the whole conversation between them and was in disbelief of what they were talking about. She laughed at what she heard. She did not joyfully laugh but it was more of a bitter laugh. How could she possibly be blessed with a child, considering her life's situation? She was way past her menopause. She married a 100-year-old husband and was homeless. Was it a fairy tale? Did she have too much wine? Did she really hear him say that?

God asked Abraham, "Why did Sarah laugh?" He called her out for sour thoughts and small-mindedness toward God's abilities, toward His promise. Even though Sarah only laughed to herself silently, God heard her loud and clear. God did not need a hearing aid to hear her laugh. God knew her desire, a baby of her own. When God asked why Sarah laughed, He had already seen her heart, and it was not pretty. When confronted, Sarah lied straight to God's face. She was afraid, and she denied it all. We could be like Sarah - old, tired, sad, and beaten down. Then we secretly laughed in mockery when we thought of blessings coming our way. We laughed in disbelief. We have begun the unraveling of faith, working the pile of loose thread into a picture of despair. But God can hear us laughing. He hears our bitter scoffing and wants to call us out on it, wanting us to come out of our inward-focused pity party.

Christmas. Sorry, I cannot stay away from Christmas! Let's talk about this woman who was a huge part of the reason for Christmas. Guess who? Any ideas? There, you! You guessed it correctly, Mary, the birth mother of Jesus. Mary was quite young when the angel came to her. She was about 13 years old. The angel Gabriel appeared to her and greeted her joyfully and pronounced her a favored woman. Young Mary was confused and disturbed, which was not surprising, seeing that this mysterious messenger was a huge, shiny nonhuman who had not been there just a second ago. Talking about being caught off guard! Gabriel told her the news, reminding her two very important yet perplexing things. "Don't be afraid," he said. "You have found favor with God." Then he slipped into a most electrifying, exalted thing a Jewish woman could ever have hoped to hear: She would be a mother of the Messiah. And oh, by the way, He would be called Son of the Most High, He would Reign over Israel forever, and the Kingdom would never end." Boom!

What?! Wait, hold up. Back up. Don't be afraid? Hey, listen, Gabe, being pregnant is scary. You get nine months of sick, tired, grumpy, itchy, chubby, swelling, and lose control of your bladder. Plus, you know like Oompa Loompa and waddle like a penguin. Oh, do not get me started on the birth! The pain, the mess, the animal smell close by…sheesh! Do not be afraid, my goodness, but by miracle, Mary did not just have, first pregnancy and birth to be afraid of. She had a truckload of obstacles ahead. She would have to face ostracism in her community as her pregnancy would appear to her to be unfaithful to her fiancé, Joseph. She faced potential stoning by her father and getting ditched by her fiancé. She could have been left in the cold, hungry, and uncared for, alone save for her promised baby boy. Mary knew there would be a hard road ahead.

The whispers and stares from the neighbors, the loss of reputation, and the responsibility of raising the very Son of God. She had every reason to be afraid. Every reason to say, “Nah, thanks, anyway, but that’s totally out of my comfort zone.” Every reason to weigh the pros and cons and go with her own plan: safe, clean, conventional, and financially beneficial plan. But she did not. She looked through the eyes of that terrifying and glorious being and asked one question: “But how can this happen? I am a virgin.” Oh, Mary, can I be you for a day? Can I just throw aside all self-preservation tendencies, all hindrance, all vanity, and earthly reasons, and just be you? She did not ask what was in it for her; she did not ask who would take care of her. She did not ask how she could hide the truth. Mary merely just wanted to know how it would even be possible.

Gabriel answered her through the Holy Spirit, and that nothing is impossible with God. Mary, in an act of worship, of truth, of devotion, of abandon, and of terrifying trust, said in Luke 1:38 (NLT) “I am the Lord’s servant.

May everything you have said about me come true." Mary said yes. When was the last time we said that to Jesus? When was the last time we looked Him in the face and said "I am Your Servant? Take me with You, Lead me into the Lion's den, King's court, and defy enemies. Risk my life for the truth. Accept my meager offering - a drink of cold water, the washing of your feet with my hair and tears, the fragrance of embalming spice pungent in the darkest hour. Take me straight to the Cross with You for I know you are good!" Mary is willing to face shame and the unknown of her life.

Mary's yes also brought blessing along with the mysterious conception of her new life. It gave Mary so much more than she could have imagined. Mary, who memorized the face of Jesus! Mary honored to tenderly change a holy diaper, washed hummus off from Jesus' full, young face, and taught him to count. Mary, who breathed in the scent of His curls and sang lullabies ever more softly so that He would lean into her warmth a bit close; Mary, fortunate to hold Jesus' small, soft hand, to teach Him the name of the animals; Mary who watched her boy grow in wisdom as He spent time in the synagogue, then witnessed His face transformed from boy to a man; Mary, privileged to witness the Gift of Heaven right under her own roof, right under her own skin; and Mary, who witnessed miracles, who followed faithfully, who stayed by Jesus' side even unto His death. Mary would have missed all this loveliness if she had chosen comfort or disobedience.

These women's stories deal with pain, yes, but thankfully also with honesty. An honesty that is crucial to healing, crucial to repentance, crucial to walking tall and strong. We all have a story. We all have tragedies and losses and heartaches and miracles and real life. While so much of life is glorious, sometimes it gets ugly. No one is exempt. We share this thing called humanity. I believe it makes the joy livelier and the laughter louder and stronger. So, bear with me, cry with me, but please, laugh with me. It is OK to cry and laugh. People still struggle with life beyond the hurt and find it hard to believe God's goodness. God knows your hurt, and He knows your name. Find security in His undeniable love and make your heart sing. Understand God's love outside circumstances and change your perspective. The Lord knew there was more for these women and even for you. There is more life in the future for you and me than a lifetime of regrets, fears, hunger, and shame. He wants us to experience high and lows, joys and sorrows, and a calling notice by self-worth and wisdom. There was forgiveness and more heart aches to come, but most of all there was a change in the future to bring God glory. A chance to encourage women to walk again, head held high with the beauty of strength, wisdom, and purpose.

God is planning to turn our mourning to joy – the kind of joy that we cannot just do ourselves, the kind of joy that requires faith in His goodness for an awesome future. It took faith to survive the impossible, nightmare days to follow. It takes faith to process the longing. It takes faith to see beyond the present sadness. It takes faith to get out of bed in the morning, faith to let your guard down. It takes faith to love someone new, faith to face another day with a destroyed and suspicious heart. It takes faith to move forward in life and truly, it takes faith to not laugh in bitterness or dwelling on the tough circumstances. The only way to get that essential faith, to experience the healing truth is to go straight to the mouth of God. It is true - faith comes from hearing and studying the Word of God. We have Heaven promised; we have redemption, joy, and comfort coming our way! We have peace and freedom and the realization of every deep desire, the unfolding of the future of the world all laid out for us. “Don’t copy the behavior and customs of this world, but let God transform you into a new person by changing the way you think. Then you will learn to know God’s will for you, which is good and pleasing and perfect.” Romans 12:2 (NLT)

Now into The Christmas Ghost of Present.

Now we have seen some of the benefits regarding having a merry heart. The question remains, how do we get a merry heart? Let’s look at Jeremiah 15:16 (KJB)

"Thy words were found, and I did eat them; and thy word was unto me, the joy and rejoicing of my heart…" God's Word is what makes our heart merry! Surprise! The more we learn about God's Word, the more we understand God's Heart for His children (that is us). We fill our hearts with the truth of God's Word and believe what the Word says because God is able and willing to perform what He had promised in His word. For example: We can REJOICE because God says that we can prosper and be in health (3 John 2). That we can TRUST in HIM (Psalm 5:11). We can PRAY to HIM and know He hears us (1 John 5:14-15). And that we can CALL upon HIM in times of trouble and He WILL deliver us (Psalm 50:15).

The Bible, His Words, rejoices our hearts, and we can read it every day - whether it is just a verse or the whole chapter. The more time we spend with God in His words, it helps us to see how our heart can be merry, and experience the sense of peace. We can rejoice in His Words, and we can be confident by knowing that God will take care of us in EVERY situation. Nothing is too difficult for God to handle. So never underestimate God. It is important to have a merry heart so it can help with controlling what and how we THINK. God lovingly gave us the ability to control our thinking; we can choose what we think. You may be asking yourself, "How can I control every thought that comes to my mind?" It is a moment-by-moment process of deciding what we hold fast to and what we get rid of. And a great key that will help us is to keep pouring on the pure truth of God's Word.

We can FILL our minds with the encouraging, gladdening, powerful promises of God, leaving no room for any negative thoughts. "Finally, brothers (sisters), whatever is true, whatever is honorable, whatever is just, whatever is pure, whatever is lovely, whatever is commendable (good/praiseworthy), if there be any excellence, if there be anything worthy of praise, think on these things." Philippians 4:8 (ESV)

As we each think about the positives of God's Word, we begin to put that Word in the innermost part of our mind. We fill our hearts with God's Word and then decide to think about the Word and believe it. What goes inside shows outside! We bring into evidence in our lives the idea and belief we hold in our hearts.

God is not finished with you yet. It is true because He is God, and you are His beloved child. When you wonder if He has forgotten you, what you are doing is questioning and even doubting His love for you.

I often forget the JOY of time spent in His presence. I have overlooked the fact that disciples must sit at the feet of the teacher like Mary, choose what is best while Martha is busy preparing dinner (Luke 10:38-42). Only in God do we discover our identity, our meaning, our purpose, and significance. So, spend time in His loving presence, while you are in His presence, forget telling Him what to do. He got it. He sees, He knows, and He does care. Jesus is waiting for you to choose what truly matters in life and that is through time spent at His feet. "And we know that all things work together for the good to those who love Him and are called according to His purpose." Romans 8:28 (NIV)

God is working behind the scenes of our lives to take every disappointment we experience and work it to our advantage. Although your heart may be hollow with the pain of an aborted dream and one downfall after another, hold on to hope. Rather than remaining in a place of disappointment, know that because of the power and love of God, nothing this side of Heaven has the capacity to "Dis"-appoint you. You have been eternally appointed for His purposes and His plans. Instead of weeping, and put yourself in discouragement and desire, you can glory in disappointment because God is still on the throne of your life. He is still in control. You have not escaped His love. He got this, He got you!

"Therefore, since we have been made right in God's sight by faith, we have peace with God because of what Jesus Christ our Lord had done for us. Because of our faith, Christ has brought us into this place of undeserved privilege where we now stand and we confidently and joyfully look forward to sharing God's glory." Romans 5:1-5 (NLT) We can rejoice, too, when we run into problems and trials, for we know that they help us develop endurance. And endurance develops strength of character, and character strengthens our confident hope of salvation. And this hope will not lead to disappointment. For we know how dearly God loves us because He has given us the Holy Spirit to fill our HEARTS with His love.

When you are overwhelmed, the first thing you need to do is cry out to God. Just going to the infinitely gracious God, who is loving and attentive in all of His ways, reminds us that we are not in charge. When you are feeling overwhelmed, begin to declare who God is. Remove your eyes from circumstances and set your mind, eyes, heart on the One and only who can help you! "O my people, trust in Him at all times, pour out your heart to HIM, for God is our refuge." Psalm 62:8 (NLT)

Do you ever wonder why God allows difficult people in your life? Difficult, frustrating people barge into our peaceful world and disrupt our stability with their instability! Why couldn't we just meet up with Santa Claus along our life journey? Why does our life seem to be filled with GRINCH? God often places difficult people in our lives not to bring out the worst in you and me but to bring out the best in us. Maybe the reason that the Lord allows our lives to collide with difficult people is not to bring out the "Selfishness" in us but to bring out the Jesus in us.

God challenged us to love the unlovable, to talk kindly about someone who had ruined our reputation with their gossip. God loves us when we are at the very worst and He calls us in every situation with every relationship to be like him. In Ephesians 5:1-2 (ESV) says, "Therefore be imitators of God, as beloved children, and walk in love, just as Christ also loved you and gave Himself up for us, an offering and a sacrifice to God as a fragrant aroma." God sent His only son, Jesus into the world because we are the difficult people who needed forgiveness and love. Do not let the difficult people steal your peace and joy.

Last but not the least - The Christmas Ghost of the Future

Let's take a look at Psalm 31:14-15 (NLT) "But I am trusting you, O Lord, saying, "You are my God!" My future is in your hands. Rescue me from those who hunt me down relentlessly." As you had already read my stories of my upbringing - the good, the bad, and the Ugly chapters of my life, and there is so much more. It is our job to simply trust in GOD. Life is not easy. I can promise you that you are not alone. You are always in *Heaven's Eyes*. He is always watching, and He knows everything … EVERYTHING that is going on in your life. "I pray that God, the source of hope, will fill you completely with joy and peace because you trust HIM. Then you will be overflowing with confident hope through the power of the Holy Spirit." Roman 15:13 (NLT)

The JOY is found wherever HE is. He is in every sunrise and sunset. His presence is visible in the first flower of spring and in the glorious leaves of fall or first snowfall in the winter. His voice is heard in the symphony of worship and in the giggle of a baby. He is found comforting widows and brokenhearted people. He is there in the humdrum of daily life when the dishes are piled up, laundry turned into mountains, and the bills never end. He is there in an unending day of loneliness and in the piles of tissues by your bed. When we are being overtaken by the truth of our emotions, what we really need is a whole lotta of Jesus. When our joy begins to fade and is replaced by loneliness or depression, we are greatly reminded by the Holy Spirit, "Sarah…Mary…Kimmy…Bill…Adien, if you are lacking joy…guess who moved?" All the joy we will ever need on this side of Heaven is found in hanging out with Jesus. It is found when we relentlessly choose more of Him and less of us. It is found when we understand the value of our intimacy with the lover of our soul and that's always through Jesus.

I understand that life is hard, and we always need to remind ourselves to experience His presence in the spite of the world that roars around me. The JOY of His presence is guaranteed to fill you to overflowing and will give you the wonderful gift of abundant life. God takes the tears of disappointment and sadness, places them with His presence, and out of that place of deep pain will erupt an abundant harvest of JOY. You are not left out of this promise. Only God can take your worst defeat, your greatest pain, and your deepest sorrow and turn it into His miraculous and JOY. Only GOD! Amen!

Future - let us not only focus on our earthly things such as today, the next hour, tomorrow, or next week. Our future is really based on where??? Everlasting life with Jesus!!! Tomorrow has not been promised to us… and today is the greatest gift that has even been given. One of my favorite verses in Philippians 4:6-7 (NLT) tells us not to "worry about ANYTHING; instead, pray about EVERYTHING." Tell God what you need and thank Him for ALL he has done. Then you will experience God's peace, which exceeds anything we can understand. His peace will guard your hearts and minds as you live in Christ Jesus." How awesome is this? Do I need to explain anymore? God wants you to pour your heart out to Him. He's got your back. He wants you to live in peace, not to worry your brain out. It really is not good for our soul, mentally and physically. Let God take your burden. The real question, are you WILLING to do that? Do you trust Him enough to let go of these "small things" and let God handle it? I feel like that person, Elsa from the movie, *Frozen*, Let it go, Let it go, cold doesn't bother me anyway. You get my point?

Chapter 15

Final Thoughts...

I want to share with you what I learned from my pastor a few years back, and it forever stuck to me. Just imagine that you have a white rope with no ending that could go on for miles. It can go across the city, across the state, across the country. It also can go around the world, twice or more. But on the beginning of the rope about a foot long, there was a tape wrapped around. Now you picture the tape on the rope. It represents your life here on earth. The rest of the rope represents eternity. What you have here on this earth is short compared to eternity-the rope that goes on and on. So where do you want to spend your eternal life? You can say, "No thanks, God, I am busy right now." Life is short. You know that. You never know when it's your last time on earth. We all picture that we would pass away when we're really, I mean REALLY, old like 100 years old. It would be a blessing if we are able to live that long. I know there are some people who do. But that is not the point of what I am trying to make. The real question, when is the good time to say, "Jesus, take me just the way I am. I am not perfect, and I cannot go in this crazy life without you. Please take my heart and make it clean. Help me see your truth and to experience your amazing grace and your everlasting love. You died on the cross so that I could have everlasting life, that I could have a placement in Eternal Heaven." Guess what? It is not too late to make that decision. I don't know about you, but I rather experience JOY and PEACE with Jesus in Heaven where there is no pain and sorrow. What about you?

Life is tough - God already told us that life will not be easy. When you do not have true joy, life will overwhelm you. Job 28:12-13 (ESV) says, "But where shall the wisdom be found? And where is the place of understanding? Man does not know its worth, and it is not found in the land of living." You can only find it through Jesus. God alone understands the top wisdom. God allows the suffering to test us, to stretch us, and expand our knowledge for His glory. It is God's purpose. Oftentimes, when we are attacked, we do not know or even understand why this happens. When you do not have the wisdom, it will destroy you. Let's read verse 28, "Behold, the fear of the Lord, that is wisdom, and to turn away from evil, is understanding." Fear of the Lord means we have the right understanding about God, about who He is, and have the right respect of God. God is saying if you want hope, joy, and peace, you must begin with the right thought and attitude of God. We must change our attitude toward God. Nothing will provide you that joy that you are looking for, only GOD. Do you have what it takes to have merry and peace in your heart? "Then the way you live will always honor and please the Lord, and your lives will produce every kind of good fruit. All the while, you will grow as you learn to know God better and better. We also pray that you will be strengthened with all his glorious power so you will have all the endurance and patience you need. May you be filled with Joy." Colossians 1:10-11.

If so, go talk with your Brothers and Sisters in Christ - "a group of [friends] who are committed to being your cheerleaders. You need other [Christians] in your life who are willing to fight for the [person] in you, even when they are fighting for the [person] in them. You don't have to have a large circle of [friends] to know the beauty of support, compassion or even tough love... you can be a good friend to one or two people, calling, texting or showing up to let them know you are in their corner. Never forget that GIFT given to you by God can also be a gift to someone else." Dukes, J. (2016) - They will be more than happy to guide you and encourage you to fellowship with others. I always enjoy fellowship with others; it is what makes us stronger. We are not alone; we are in this together. "Two people are better off than one, for they can help each other succeed. If one person falls, the other can reach out and help. But someone who falls alone is in real trouble." Ecclesiastes 4:9-10 (NLT) Amen.

We need each other to uplift one another and to give each other support. There is never a mistake in

Heaven's Eyes. He knew exactly what He was doing. He indeed loves each one of you. You are important to Him. He just wants you to spend time with Him. Come on; let us have a coffee with Jesus. We take one thought at a time, line it up with what God says, and believe in HIS words, because our Heavenly Father provides for all the needs of HIS children. That is US, so we too can experience peace in our hearts.

They want God's gifts, but they do not want a deeper communion with God. What a difference it would make if they would only surrender themselves to the Lord and focus on the Giver instead of the gifts! In the book of John 14, verse 23-24 (NLT), it says, "Jesus replied, "All who love me will do what I say. My Father will love them and we will come and make our home with each of them. Anyone who doesn't love me will not obey me. And remember, my words are not my own. What I am telling you is from the Father who sent me." "So if only we will commit ourselves to Him. Not only in your church, but also in your home, your neighborhood, your place of employment, your school, even your sickroom, God can use you to influence others and accomplish His purposes, if only you are fully committed to Him." Wiersbe, W. (1993)

The real question, what are you going to do about it? Are you going to just keep his gifts and not spend time with the giver? When was the last time you paused from the busyness of life and just talked with Jesus? He is waiting for you. If you have not in a while, please do not wait. Now would be a perfect time before it is too late. You do not know when your days are numbered. It could be 10 years, 50 years, next month, next week, or it could happen tomorrow. So why not take a pause and talk, ask him to come into your life. No matter how much baggage you have, or how messy your life looks. God did not say, "Come to me when you are perfectly clean." No, He never did. Jesus said, "Come to me, all of you who are weary and carry heavy burdens, and I WILL give you rest." Matthew 11:28 (NIV)

God knows what is best for you. My life, as you just read, was not perfect. It was surely a bumpy ride, but God was with me, and He will always be. How awesome is that? To be able to breathe and know that whatever life experience you encounter, you are not ALONE. Jesus wanted you to cast or throw your burdens to Him. He did not want you to carry this heavy load by yourself. So, take the time to walk and talk with Jesus before it is too late. This was and will always be the best decision I have ever made, and I pray that you would do the same.

I loved how the author Jennifer Duke Lee stated in one of her books, "Let's not forget to take a moment to say Thank you, Lord, because despite everything, this old world is still a beautiful place. No matter how hopeless it all seems, there's always, ALWAYS something to be THANKFUL for." (2016)

Dear Lord,

I just wanted to take a moment to say Thank You, for loving me just the way I am. Thank you for showing your love to this unlovely child. I never thought I would have written this book. I could have not done this without you, Lord. Thank you for bringing so many wonderful people into my life. Because In Heaven's Eyes, I know and I strongly believe that you will do the same for others in your own time. Lord, I pray that you would touch their heart, mind, and their soul just like you have done to mine. I also pray for those who are hurting, struggling, and experiencing heartbreaking situations, let them know that they are WORTHY and LOVED by you Lord. Thank You for your wonderful gift - the Son Jesus who died for us which we do not deserve, but You did so because You first loved us and saw the Light at the end of the tunnel. Please forgive us for not pausing during our crazy, busy life and pause to spend time with you. Help us to be more like you and to focus on the most important thing in life and that is YOU. Thank You,

Your Daughter -
Kimberly

Citations:

1. Dukes, J (2016) *The Happiness Dare*. Carol Stream, IL:

2.Tyndale House Publishers, Inc. Hurst, C. (2017). *She's Still There*. Grand Rapids, MI:

3.Wierbe, Warren W. (1993) page 182. *Be Committed OT Commentary. Ruthe/Esther. Colorodo, Springs,* CO: David Cook, 2007. Print. Second Edition 2008

4. deafstars.deafnewspaper.com, Kovacs, May 29, 2017; Jonathan Kovacs.

Kimberly A. Snipe, Author

Prosperity Publishing Company
www.prosperitypublishingcompany.com